BASICS OF KEYBOARD THEORY

LEVEL 9

Sixth Edition

Julie McIntosh Johnson

J. Johnson Music Publications
P.O. Box 230
Lockwood, CA 93932
Phone: (714) 961-0257
Fax: (714) 242-9350
www.bktmusic.com
info@bktmusic.com

Sixth Edition ©2019, Julie McIntosh Johnson
Previous Editions © 1983, 1993, 1997, 2007, 2014, Julie McIntosh Johnson

Basics of Keyboard Theory, Level 9, Sixth Edition

Published by:

J. Johnson Music Publications
P.O. Box 230
Lockwood, CA 93932 U.S.A.
(714) 961-0257
www.bktmusic.com

All rights reserved. No part of this book may be reproduced or transmitted in any form or by any means, electronic or mechanical, including photocopying, recording, or by any information storage and retrieval system without written permission from the author, except for the inclusion of brief quotations in a review.

©2019 by Julie McIntosh Johnson. Revised.
Previous editions ©1983, 1993, 1997, 2007, 2014, Julie McIntosh Johnson.
Printed in United States of America

Library of Congress Cataloging in Publication Data

Johnson, Julie Anne McIntosh
Basics of Keyboard Theory, Level 9, Sixth Edition

ISBN 10: 1-891757-37-7
ISBN 13: 978-1-891757-37-2
LC TX 4-721-491

TO THE TEACHER

Intended as a supplement to private or group music lessons, *Basics of Keyboard Theory, Level 9* presents basic theory concepts to the advanced music student. This level is to be used with the student who has had approximately 9-10 years of music lessons, and is playing piano literature at the level of Mozart's Piano Sonatas, or Chopin's Waltzes.

Basics of Keyboard Theory, Level 9 is divided into twenty-three lessons, plus two multi-chapter reviews and a final test. Application of each theory concept is made to piano music of the student's level. Lessons may be combined with one another or divided into smaller sections, depending on the ability of the student. Whenever possible, it is helpful to demonstrate theory concepts on the keyboard and apply them to the music the student is playing.

Learning music theory can be a very rewarding experience for the student when carefully applied to lessons. *Basics of Keyboard Theory, Level 9,* is an important part of learning this valuable subject.

Basics of Keyboard Theory, Level 9 corresponds with the MTAC Certificate of Merit® Piano Syllabus. Certificate of Merit® is an evaluation program of the Music Teachers' Association of California. Reference to 'Certificate of Merit®' (CM) does not imply endorsement by MTAC of this product.

Ear Training Basics
Levels Preparatory through 10

by
Julie Johnson
Author of *Basics of Keyboard Theory*

- An innovative teaching approach helps minimize student guessing.
- Separate student and teacher books provide the framework for a collaborative learning experience.
- Teacher Books include activities to be completed at the lesson, teaching tips, and answers for the student home assignments.
- Student Books include worksheets and an MP3 CD.

www.bktmusic.com

J. Johnson Music Publications
info@bktmusic.com

Julie Johnson's Guide to AP* Music Theory, Second Edition

- Follows requirements of the College Board Advanced Placement* Music Theory exam
- Edited and expanded based on customer feedback
- More progressive sight-singing and ear-training
- New In-Class ear-training pages for instructor and student collaboration
- More "free response" assignments
- Practice test and grading guidelines
- Supplementary materials available online
- Downloadable audio files at www.juliejohnsontheory.com

*AP and Advanced Placement are trademarks registered and/or owned by the College Board, which was not involved in the production of, and does not endorse, this product.

TABLE OF CONTENTS

Lesson 1: Major and Minor Key Signatures..1

Lesson 2: Scales and Modes..13

Lesson 3: Intervals..21

Lesson 4: Diatonic and Chromatic Half Steps..25

Lesson 5: Major, Minor, Augmented, and Diminished Triads and Inversions................................29

Lesson 6: Primary and Secondary Triads; Figured Bass...37

Lesson 7: Seventh Chords...47

Lesson 8: The Secondary Dominant...55

Lesson 9: Authentic, Half, Plagal, and Deceptive Cadences; Chord Progressions..........................61

Lesson 10: Modulation..69

Review: Terms Used in Lessons 1-10...75

Review: Lessons 1-10...77

Lesson 11: Time Signatures...87

Lesson 12: Homophonic and Polyphonic Textures..97

Lesson 13: Contrapuntal Techniques..101

Lesson 14: The Fugue..111

Lesson 15: Dances of the Baroque Suite..119

Lesson 16: Sonata Form..125

Lesson 17: Signs and Terms..135

Lesson 18: Transposition..147

Lesson 19: The Four Periods of Music History; The Baroque Period; Corelli, Purcell, and Rameau..151

Lesson 20: The Classical Period; Beethoven, Haydn, and Mozart..157

Lesson 21: The Romantic Period; Brahms, Liszt, and Tchaikovsky..163

Lesson 22: Impressionism in Music; Debussy, Ravel, Griffes...169

Lesson 23: The 20th and 21st Centuries; Copland, Ives, Gershwin..173

Review: Lessons 11-23...179

Review Test..187

Basics of Keyboard Theory is dedicated to my husband Rob,
without whose love, support, help, and incredible patience,
this series would not have been possible.

LESSON 1
MAJOR AND MINOR KEY SIGNATURES

The **KEY SIGNATURE** for a musical composition is found at the beginning of the music, between the clef and the time signature.

The **KEY SIGNATURE** indicates the following:

1. The **key** or **tonality** of the music.

2. Which notes receive sharps or flats.

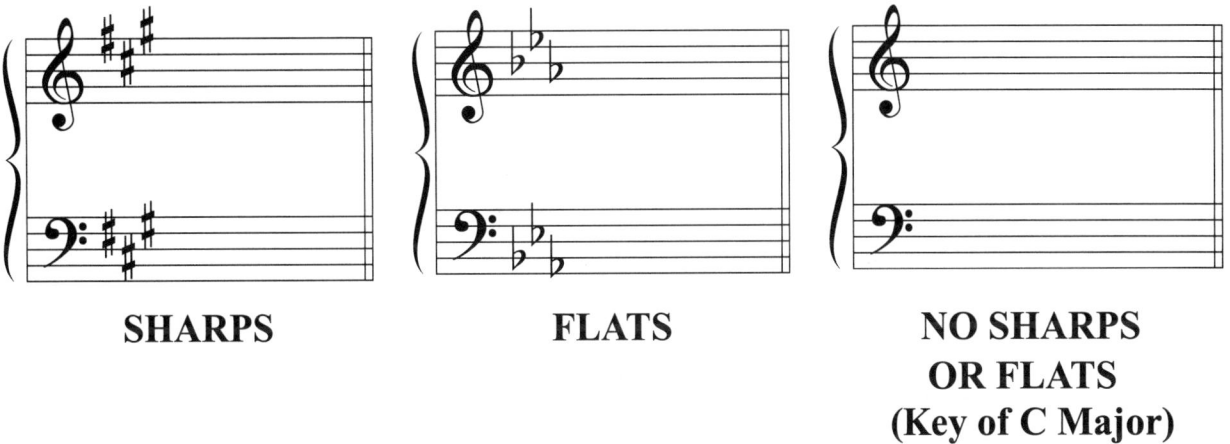

SHARPS **FLATS** **NO SHARPS OR FLATS (Key of C Major)**

If the key signature has <u>SHARPS</u>, they will be written in this order, on these lines and spaces. This is called the **ORDER OF SHARPS**.

THE ORDER OF SHARPS

A saying to help you remember this order is:

Fat Cats Go Down Alleys Eating Bologna

If a key signature has one sharp, it will be F♯. If a key signature has two sharps, they will be F♯ and C♯, etc.

To determine which Major key a group of sharps represents, find and name the last sharp (the sharp furthest to the right), then go up a half step. The note which is a half step above the last sharp is the name of the Major key.

Three sharps: F♯, C♯, G♯

Last sharp is G♯

A half step above G♯ is A

Key of A Major

To determine which sharps are in a Major key, find the sharp which is a half step below the name of the key. Name all the sharps from the Order of Sharps up to and including that sharp.

Key of D Major

A half step below D is C♯

Name all sharps, from the Order of Sharps, up to and including C♯

F♯ and C♯

If a key signature has <u>FLATS</u>, they will be in the following order, written on these lines and spaces. This is called the **ORDER OF FLATS.**

BEADGCF

THE ORDER OF FLATS

The Order of Flats can be memorized this way:

BEAD Gum Candy Fruit

If a key signature has one flat, it will be B♭. If it has two flats, they will be B♭ and E♭, etc.

To determine which Major key a group of flats represents, name the next to last flat.

Three flats: B♭, E♭, A♭

Next to last flat is E♭

Key of E♭ Major

To determine which flats are needed for a given key, name all the flats from the Order of Flats up to and including the name of the key, then add one more.

Key of E♭ Major

Name all flats from the Order of Flats up to and including E♭, then add one more.

B♭, E♭, A♭

The key signature for F Major is an exception. It has one flat: B♭.

KEY SIGNATURE FOR F MAJOR

Major keys which have sharps will be named with a letter, or a letter and a sharp (for example, G Major, D Major, F♯ Major).

Major keys which have flats will have a flat in their names (for example, B♭ Major, D♭ Major, E♭ Major).

The two exceptions are F Major (one flat: B♭), and C Major (no sharps or flats).

1. Name each of the following Major keys.

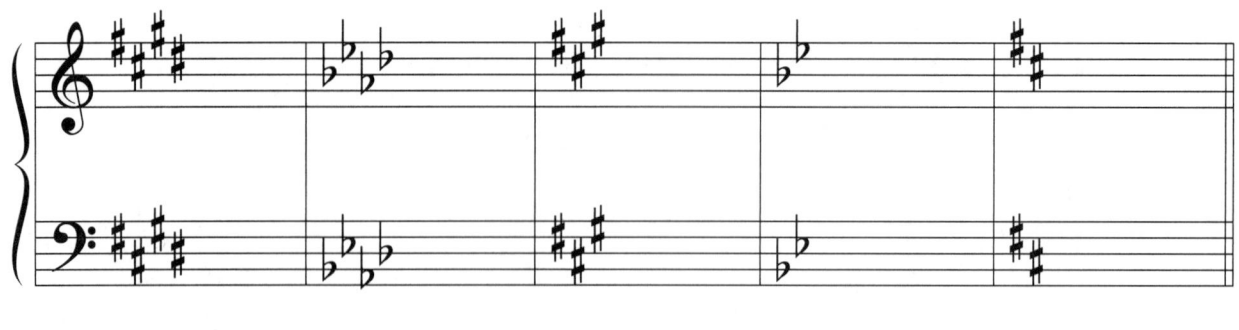

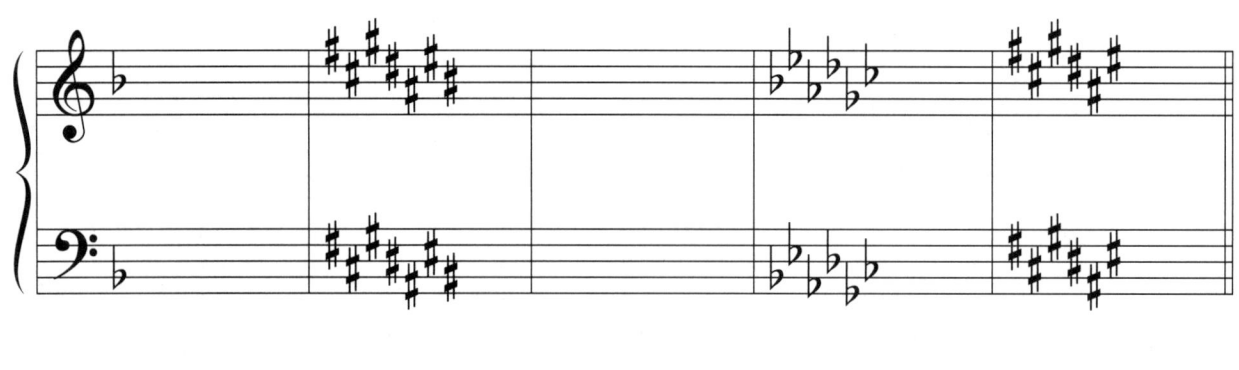

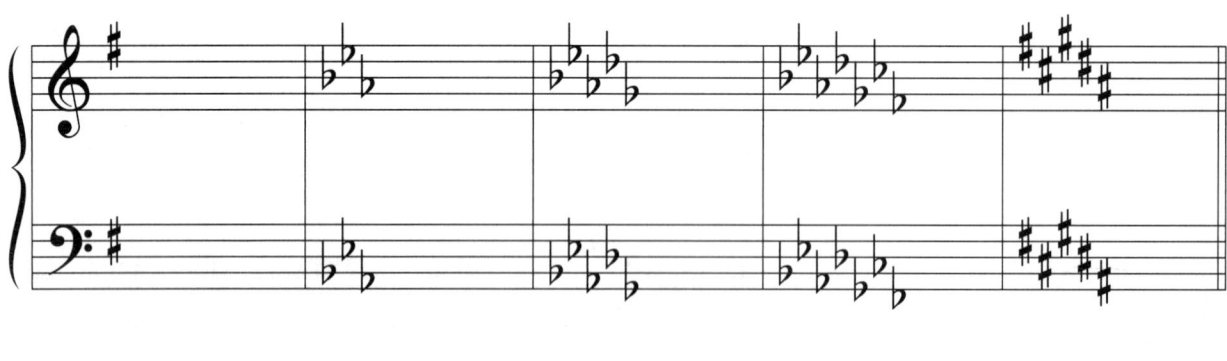

2. Notate the key signature for each of the following Major keys in both clefs.

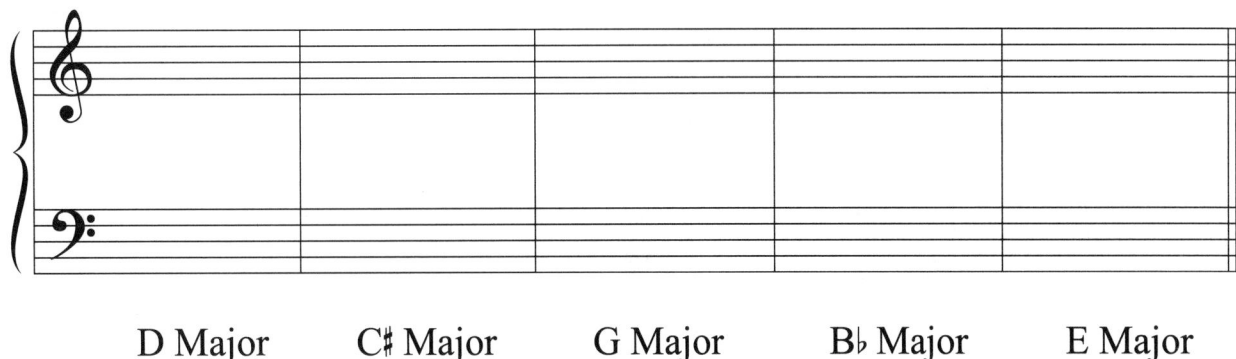

D Major   C♯ Major   G Major   B♭ Major   E Major

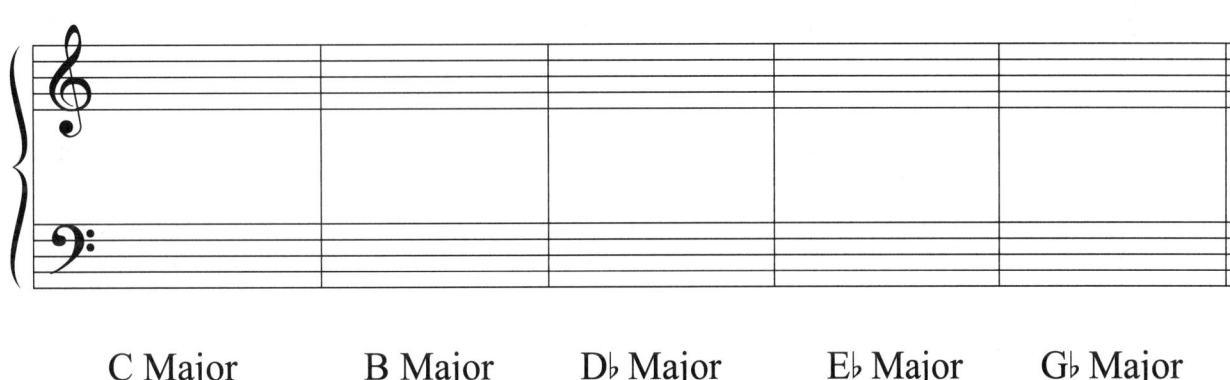

C Major   B Major   D♭ Major   E♭ Major   G♭ Major

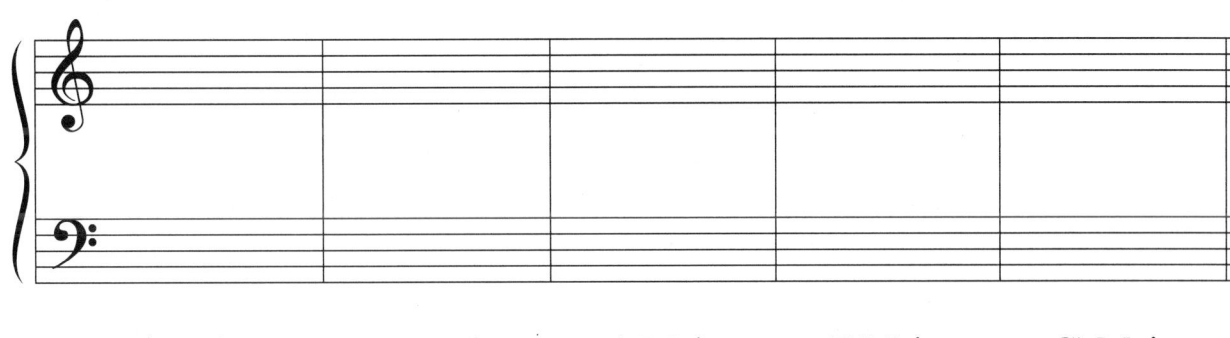

F♯ Major   A♭ Major   A Major   F Major   C♭ Major

Many Major keys have **RELATIVE MINORS**. The relative minor is found by going down three half steps from the name of the Major key. Skip one letter between the names of the keys.

KEY SIGNATURE FOR D MAJOR
THREE HALF STEPS BELOW D IS B
KEY OF B MINOR

PARALLEL MAJOR AND MINOR KEYS have the same letter name, such as C Major and c minor.

One way to determine whether a composition is in the Major or minor key is to look at the last note of the music. It is usually the same as the name of the key. (For example, if the music is in the key of e minor will probably end on E.) Also, look at the music to find the note upon which the music appears to be based (the "tonal center"). This should be the same as the name of the key.

3. Name each of the following <u>minor</u> keys.

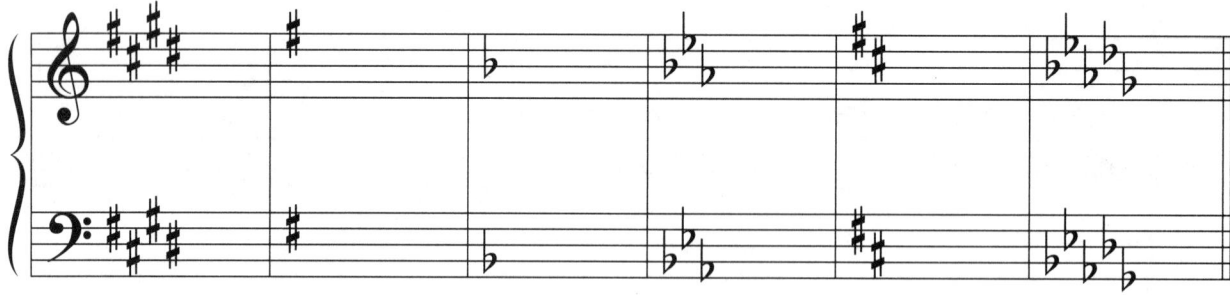

_____ _____ _____ _____ _____ _____

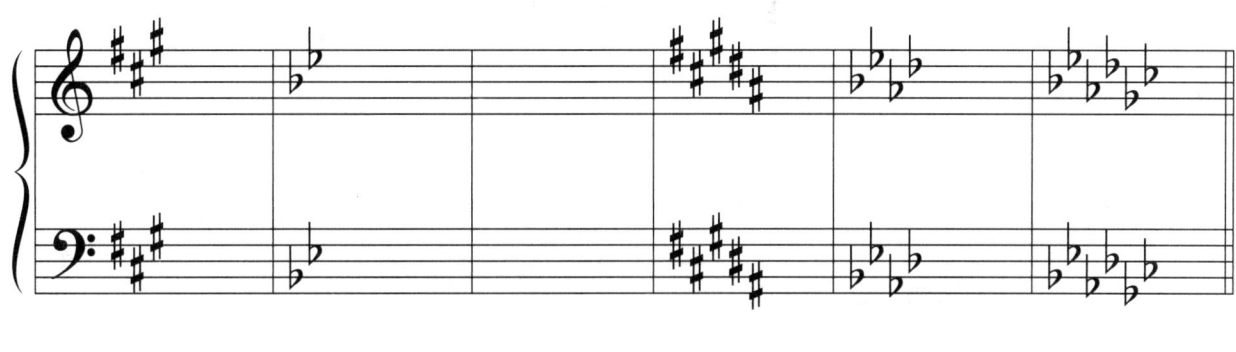

_____ _____ _____ _____ _____ _____

4. Notate the key signature for each of the following minor keys in both clefs.

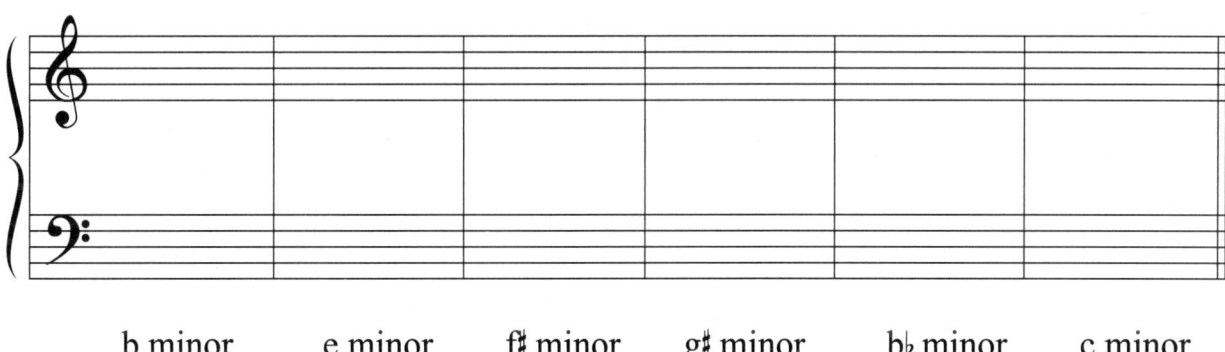

b minor   e minor   f# minor   g# minor   b♭ minor   c minor

a minor   c# minor   d minor   g minor   f minor   e♭ minor

5. Write the name of the Major or minor key for each of the following excerpts.

a. From *Invention No. 14* by J.S. Bach. _____ _____

b. From *Sonata, Op. 14, No. 1* by Beethoven. _____ _____

c. From *Nocturne, Op. posth. 72, No. 1,* by Chopin. _____ _____

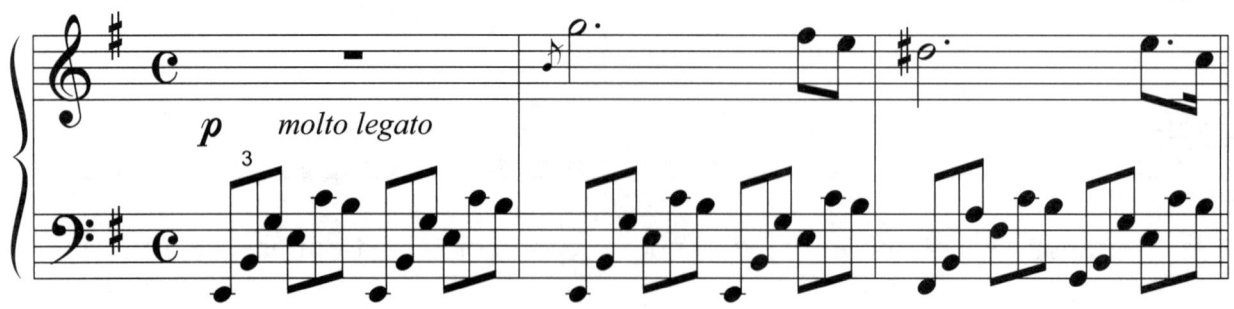

d. From *Rhapsody, Op. 119, No. 4,* by Brahms. _____ _____

e. From *Sonata, Hob. XVI:19,* by Haydn. _____ _____

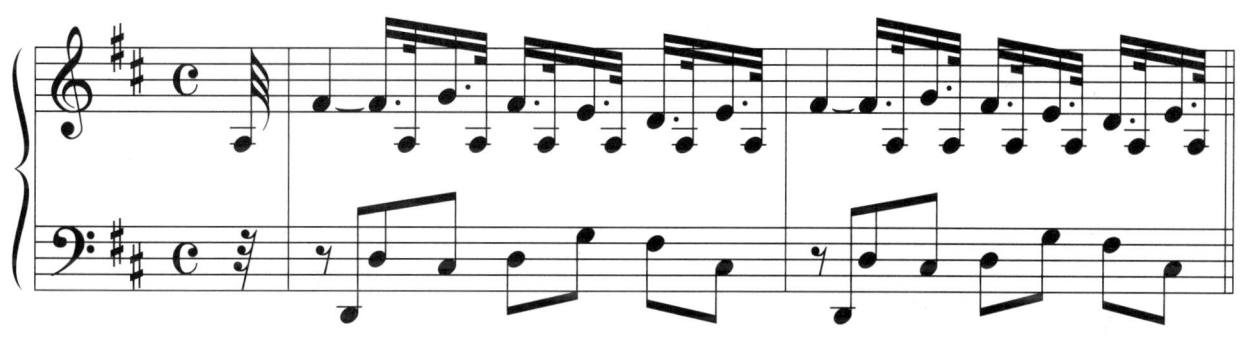

f. From *Sinfonia No. 9* by J.S. Bach. _____ _____

g. From *Sonata No. 31* by Scarlatti. _____ _____

h. From *Sonata, Op. 10, No. 1,* by Beethoven. _____ _____

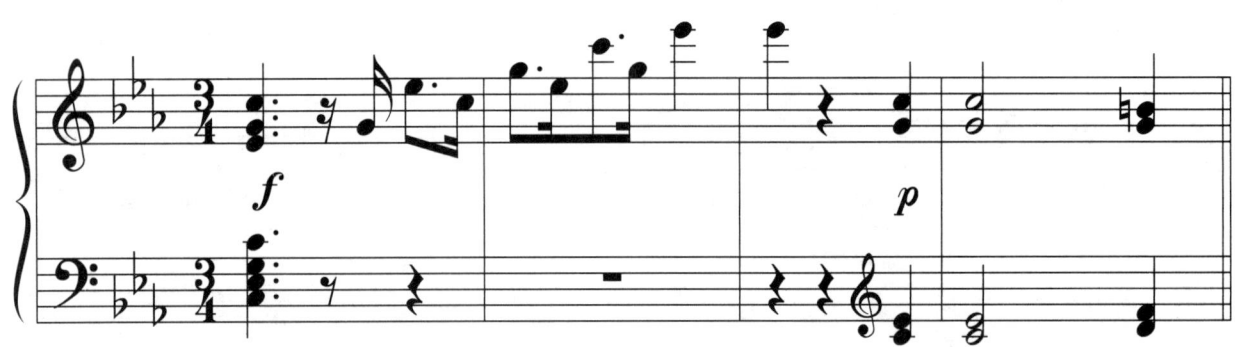

i. From *The Wanderer, Op. 30, No. 4,* by Mendelssohn. _____ _____

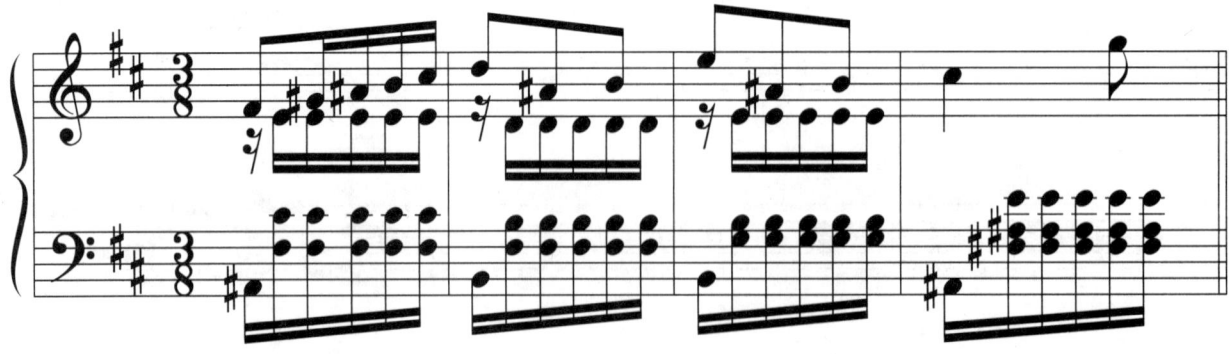

The **CIRCLE OF FIFTHS** (sometimes called the **Circle of Keys**) is a method of organizing the Major and minor keys so that when ascending by perfect fifths from key to key, one sharp is added to each new key. When the keys of B, F♯, and C♯ are reached, there is an <u>enharmonic</u> change (notes with the same pitch but different letter names, such as F♯ and G♭). Flats are then used, and as the keys ascend by perfect fifths, one flat is deleted from each key.

*The Circle of Fifths may also be referred to as the Circle of Fourths. Moving counterclockwise through the chart demonstrates the Circle of Fourths.

6. Fill in the Circle of Fifths (Circle of Keys) below. Include the Major and minor key names and the enharmonic equivalents, and notate each key signature on the staff.

LESSON 2
SCALES AND MODES

<u>**SCALES**</u> are an organized sequence of notes upon which a composition is based.

MAJOR SCALES contain seven different pitches (when performed the first pitch is repeated at the end of the scale), and have the same sharps or flats as the Major key signature with the same name. <u>**IONIAN MODE**</u> has the same pattern of whole and half steps as the major scale.

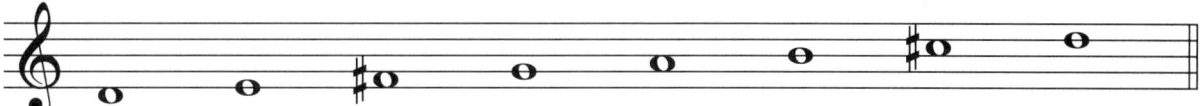

D MAJOR SCALE or IONIAN MODE

<u>**NATURAL MINOR SCALES**</u> contain all the sharps or flats from the minor key signature with the same name. Example: d natural minor scale begins and ends with the note "D," and has B♭. <u>**AEOLIAN MODE**</u> has the same pattern of whole and half steps as the natural minor scale.

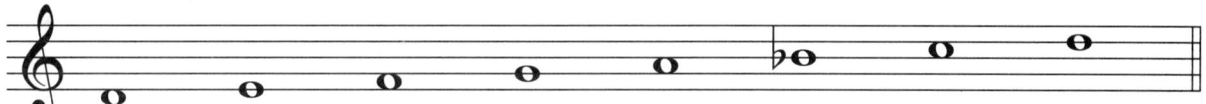

D NATURAL MINOR SCALE or AEOLIAN MODE

<u>**HARMONIC MINOR SCALES**</u> are created by raising the seventh note of the natural minor scale a half step. This creates a half step, rather than a whole step, between the seventh and eighth notes of the scale, making the seventh a "leading tone."

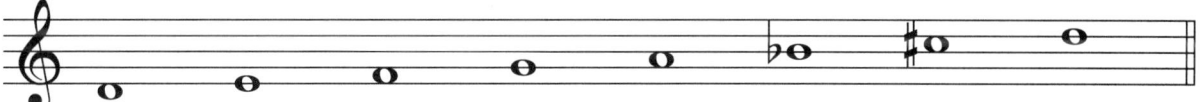

D HARMONIC MINOR SCALE

<u>**MELODIC MINOR SCALES**</u> are created by raising the sixth and seventh notes of the natural minor scale while ascending, and returning them to natural minor (lowering them) while descending.

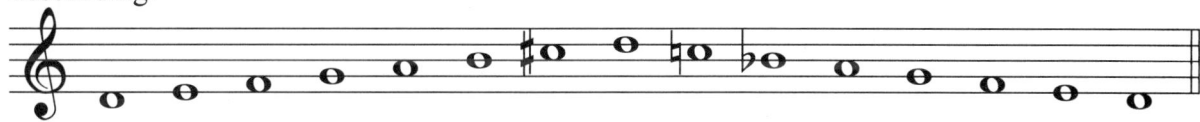

D MELODIC MINOR SCALE

The <u>**CHROMATIC SCALE**</u> includes all twelve pitches. Each note is a half step away from its neighbor. Using sharps while the scale is ascending and flats while the scale is descending avoids the use of many naturals and makes the scale easier to read, but is not required.

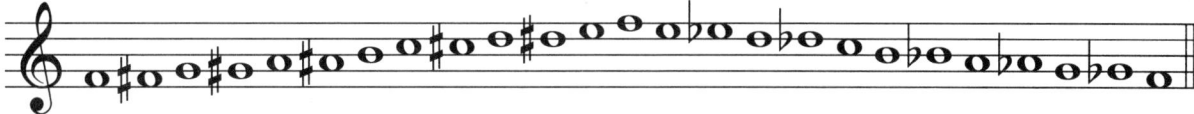

CHROMATIC SCALE BEGINNING ON F

The **WHOLE TONE SCALE** consists entirely of whole steps. When writing the scale on the staff, one letter name will be missing.

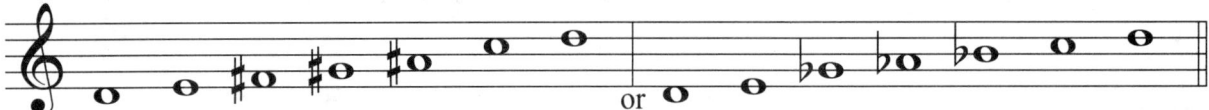

DORIAN MODE contains the pattern of whole and half steps that occurs when beginning and ending on the **SECOND** note of the major scale. Half steps occur between notes 2-3 and 6-7. The major scale becomes Dorian by lowering the third and seventh scale degrees a half step.

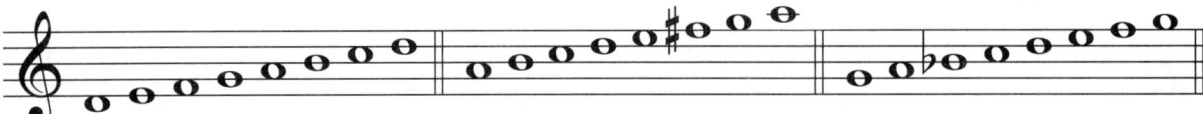

PHRYGIAN MODE contains the pattern of whole and half steps that occurs when beginning and ending on the **THIRD** note of the major scale. Half steps occur between notes 1-2 and 5-6. The major scale becomes Phrygian by lowering the second, third, sixth, and seventh scale degrees a half step.

LYDIAN MODE contains the pattern of whole and half steps that occurs when beginning and ending on the **FOURTH** note of the major scale. Half steps occur between notes 4-5 and 7-8. The major scale becomes Lydian by raising the fourth scale degree a half step.

MIXOLYDIAN MODE contains the pattern of whole and half steps that occurs when beginning and ending on the **FIFTH** note of the major scale. Half steps occur between notes 3-4 and 6-7. The major scale becomes Mixolydian by lowering the seventh scale degree a half step.

AEOLIAN MODE contains the pattern of whole and half steps that occurs when beginning and ending on the **SIXTH** note of the major scale. Half steps occur between notes 2-3 and 5-6. The major scale becomes Aeolian by lowering the third, sixth, and seventh scale degrees a half step. It is the same as the natural minor scale.

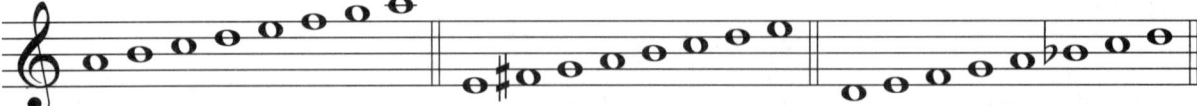

LOCRIAN MODE contains the pattern of whole and half steps that occurs when beginning and ending on the **SEVENTH** note of the major scale. Half steps occur between notes 1-2 and 4-5. The major scale becomes Locrian by lowering the second, third, fifth, sixth and seventh scale degrees a half step.

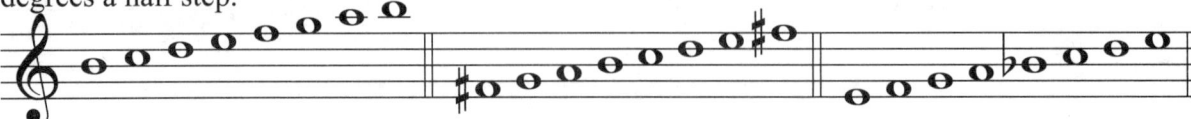

Name of Mode	Major Scale Degree:	Interval to Descend to Find Key Signature	Locations of Half-Steps	Scale Degree Changes
Ionian	1	None	3-4 7-8	None
Dorian	2	M2	2-3 6-7	3 and 7 Lowered
Phrygian	3	M3	1-2 5-6	2, 3, 6, and 7 Lowered
Lydian	4	P4	4-5 7-8	4 Raised
Mixolydian	5	P5	3-4 6-7	7 Lowered
Aeolian	6	M6	2-3 5-6	3, 6, and 7 Lowered
Locrian	7	M7	1-2 4-5	2, 3, 5, 6, & 7 Lowered

To determine which sharps or flats are in a mode:

Starting with the letter name of the mode, go down the interval listed in the third column of the above chart. Use the key signature for that note.

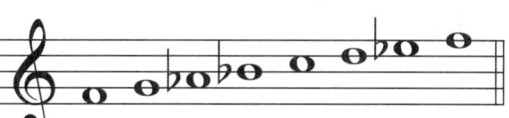

Dorian Mode on F
Go down a M2 below F
Use E♭ Major Key Signature

To determine the name of a mode:

Look at the accidentals and determine the Major key signature that uses them

Count up from the name of that Major key to the starting note of the mode

Match the name of the mode with the associated scale degree

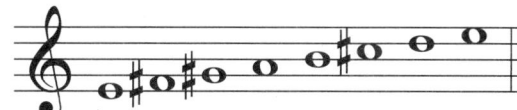

Sharps are F♯, C♯, G♯
A Major key signature
E is the fifth note of A Major
Mixolydian Mode

1. Notate each of the following scales using accidentals (not key signatures).

C♯ Major

b natural minor

Chromatic beginning on B (ascending and descending)

f harmonic minor

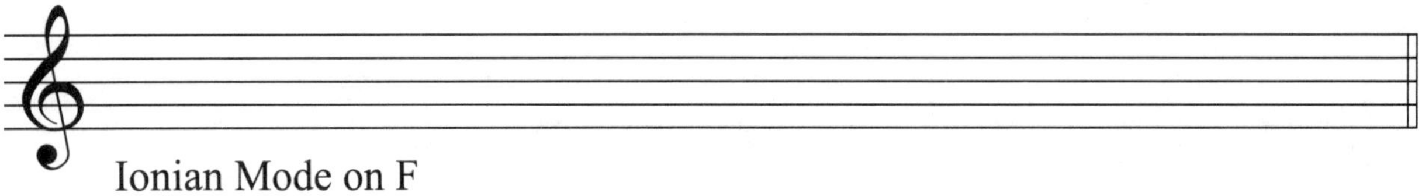

18

Ionian Mode on F

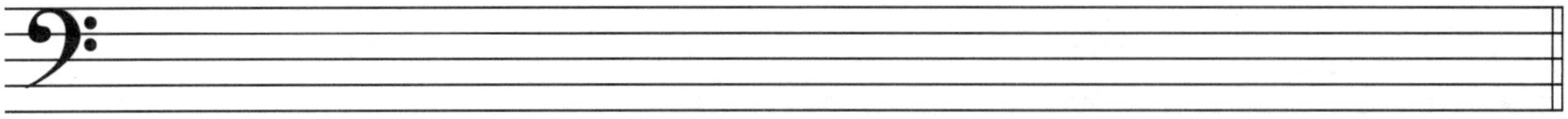

Mixolydian Mode on D

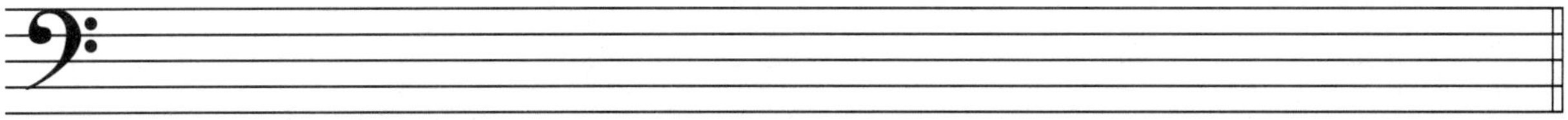

Lydian Mode on C

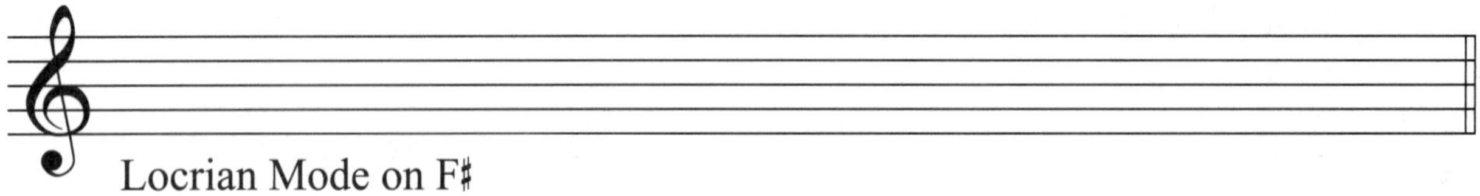

Locrian Mode on F♯

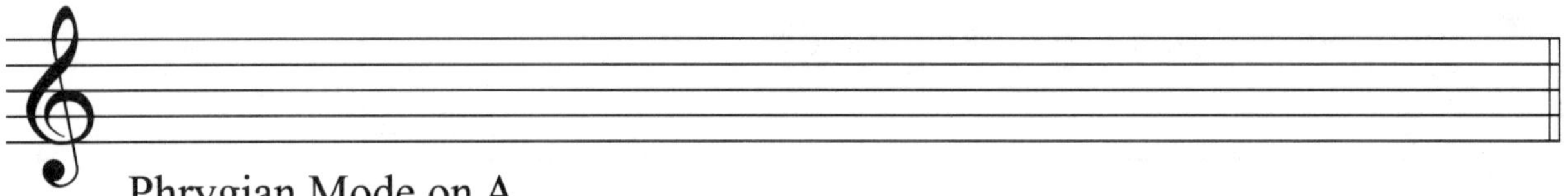

Phrygian Mode on A

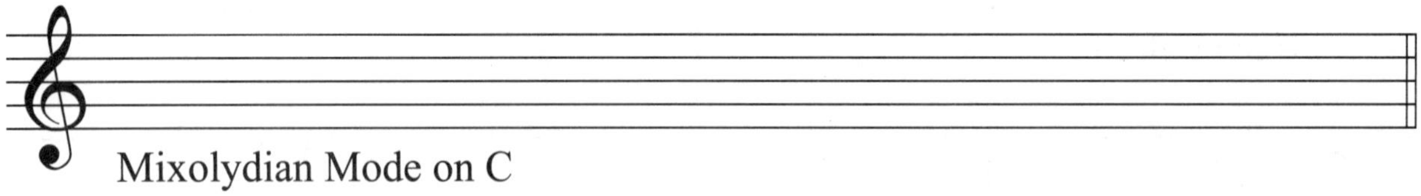

Mixolydian Mode on C

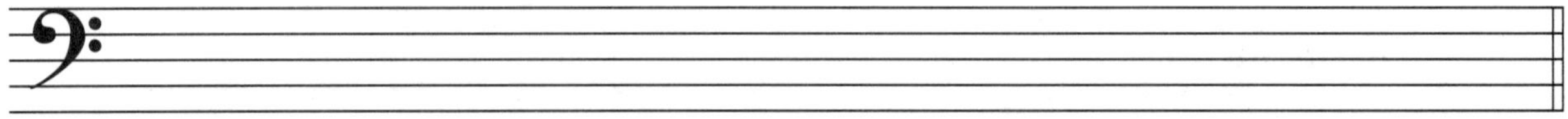

Lydian Mode on B♭

2. For each of the following phrases, write the name and type of scale upon which the music is based. For minor scales, include the form of minor.

a. From *French Suite No. 1: Menuet,* by J.S. Bach. _____ Scale

20

f. From *Sonata, XVI:40* by Haydn. _____ Scale

g. From *Invention No. 4* by J.S. Bach. _____ Scale

h. From *Sonata, XVI:40,* by Haydn. _____ Scale

i. From *Sonata, XVI:42,* by Haydn. _____ Scale

LESSON 3
INTERVALS

An **INTERVAL** is the distance between two notes. Intervals are named with qualities and numbers. When naming intervals, count the two notes that create the interval, and all the letter names between the two.

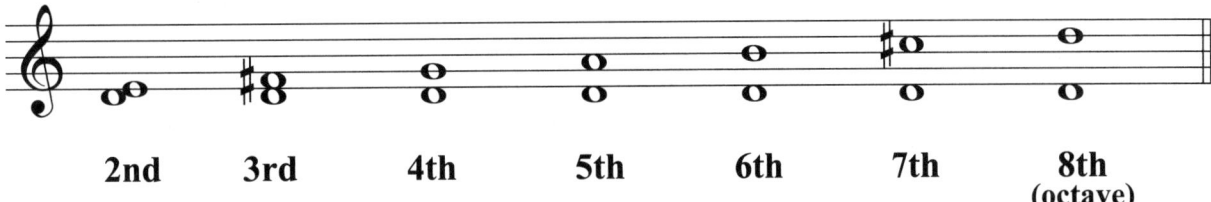

2nd   3rd   4th   5th   6th   7th   8th (octave)

If the top note of the interval is within the key of the bottom note, the interval is **Major** or **Perfect**. 2nds, 3rds, 6ths, and 7ths are Major. 4ths, 5ths, and octaves (8ths) are perfect.

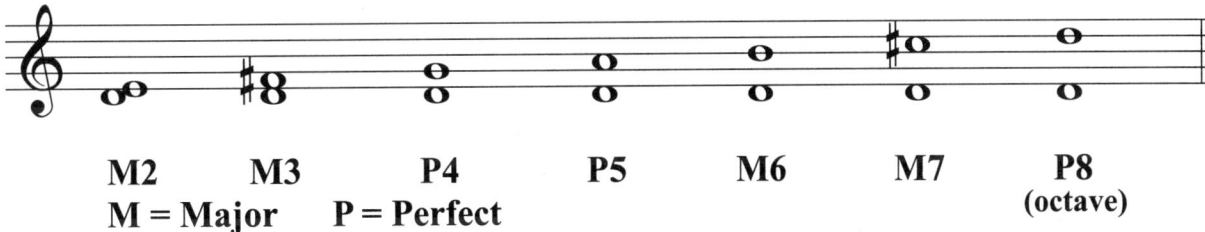

M2   M3   P4   P5   M6   M7   P8 (octave)

M = Major   P = Perfect

If a Major 2nd, 3rd, 6th, or 7th is made smaller by lowering the top note or raising the bottom note a half step, without changing the letter name of either note, the interval becomes **minor**.

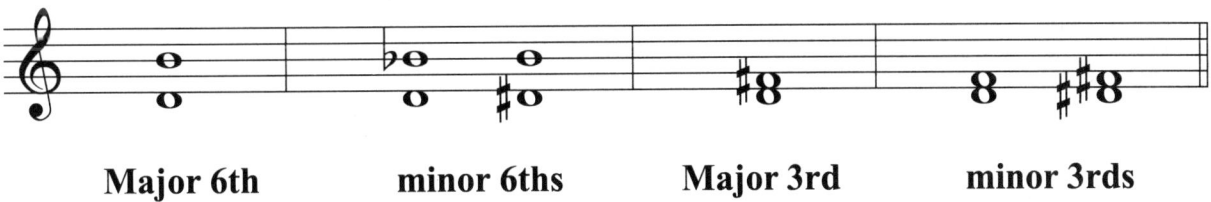

Major 6th   minor 6ths   Major 3rd   minor 3rds

If a Perfect 4th, 5th, or octave is made smaller by lowering the top note or raising the bottom note a half step, without changing the letter name of either note, the interval becomes **diminished**.

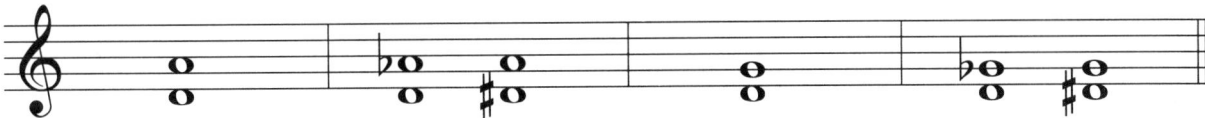

Perfect 5th   diminished 5ths   Perfect 4th   diminished 4ths

If a Major 2nd, 3rd, 6th, or 7th is made smaller by lowering the top note or raising the bottom note a whole step, without changing the letter name of either note, the interval becomes **diminished**.

Major 6th   diminished 6ths

If a Major or Perfect interval is made larger by raising the top note or lowering the bottom note a half step, without changing the letter name of either note, the interval becomes **Augmented.**

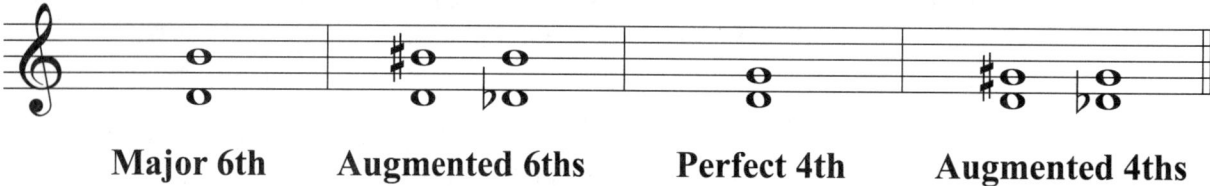

Major 6th   Augmented 6ths   Perfect 4th   Augmented 4ths

To draw an interval above a note:

1. Determine the key signature for the lower note.
2. Add any accidentals from the key signature to the upper note.
3. For Major or Perfect intervals, keep those accidentals.
   For minor, diminished, or Augmented intervals, raise or lower the top note without changing the letter name.

To draw an interval below a note:

1. Determine all possibilities the note could be.
2. Determine which of those notes is the correct one for the quality of the interval.

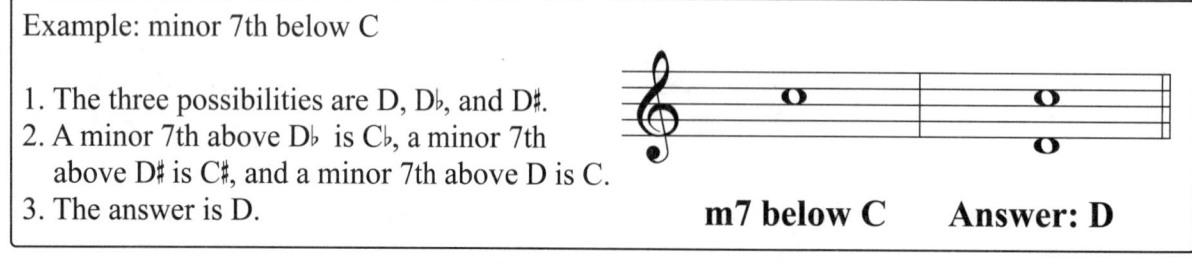

1. Name each of the following intervals with its quality and number.

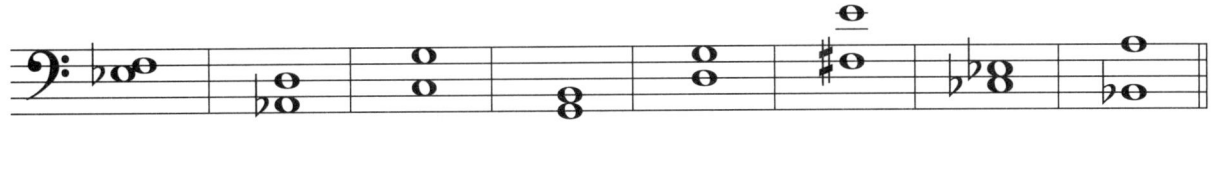

____ ____ ____ ____ ____ ____ ____

____ ____ ____ ____ ____ ____ ____

2. Complete each of the following intervals. Do note change the given note.

A2 up   m6 down   d7 up   A5 down   A7 up   A8 up   M6 down   m6 down

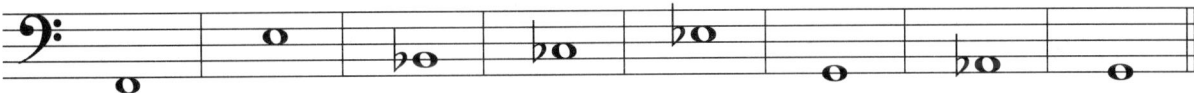

d4 up   M6 down   A3 down   M7 up   d8 down   M2 up   P5 up   m3 up

To name an interval within a composition:

a. Draw the sharps or flats from the key signature or from earlier in the measure before the notes as reminders.

b. Determine the number for the interval by counting the lines and spaces or the letter names.

c. Using the **key signature for the low note of the interval**, determine the quality (Major, minor, Perfect, diminished, or Augmented).

3. Name the circled intervals in each of the following phrases.

a. From *Nocturne, Op. posth. 72, No. 1,* by Chopin.

_____ _____ _____ _____ _____

b. From *Sonata, XVI:19,* by Haydn.

_____ _____ _____ _____

c. From *Sinfonia No. 3* by J.S. Bach.

_____ _____ _____ _____

LESSON 4
DIATONIC AND CHROMATIC HALF STEPS

Music is **DIATONIC** when it is based on the Major scale or any form of minor scale.

Music is **CHROMATIC** when it is based on the chromatic scale.

Any half-step that is formed by two notes with the same letter name is a **CHROMATIC HALF-STEP.**

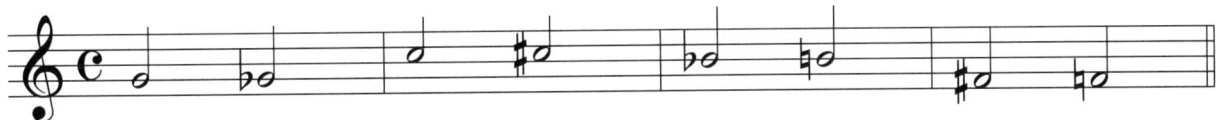

CHROMATIC HALF-STEPS

There are two schools of thought regarding half-steps that are formed by two different letter names.

Definition 1:

A **DIATONIC HALF-STEP** is one that occurs naturally within the scale.

A **CHROMATIC HALF-STEP** is one that does not occur naturally within the scale.

Example in the key of D Major:
F♯ to G and C♯ to D occur naturally within the D Major scale. These are diatonic half-steps. All other half-steps are chromatic, whether notated using two different letter names or using the same letter name.

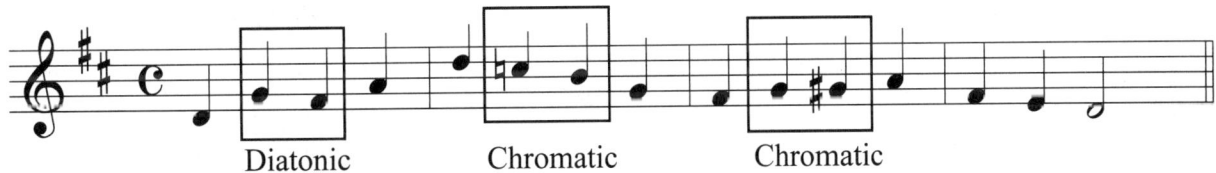

Definition 2:

A **DIATONIC HALF-STEP** is any half-step which is formed by notes with two different letter names.

A **CHROMATIC HALF-STEP** is any half-step that is formed by notes of the same letter name.

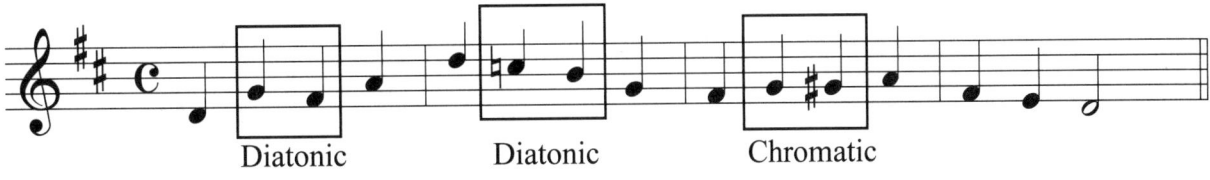

Certificate of Merit® requirements no longer include diatonic and chromatic half-steps.

1. Notate diatonic half steps above each of the following notes, using two different letter names.

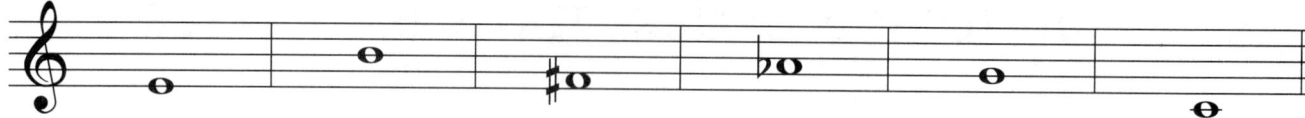

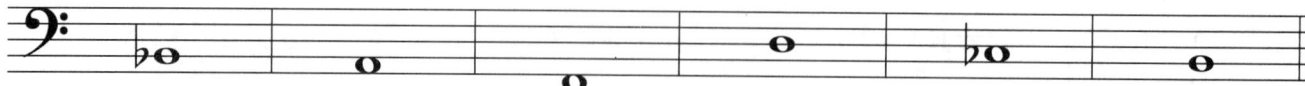

2. Notate chromatic half-steps above each of the following notes, using the same letter name.

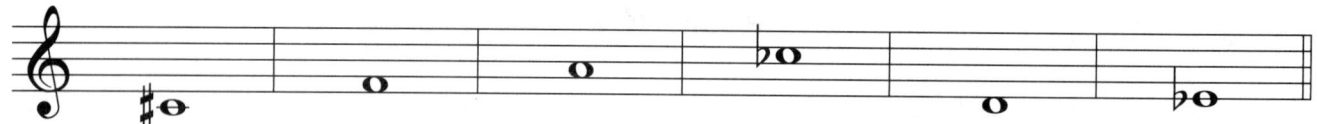

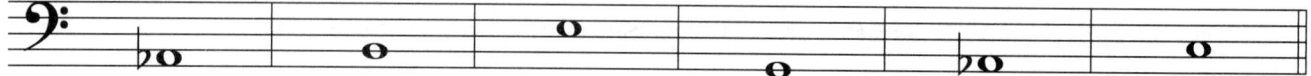

To determine whether a half-step that is formed by two different letter names is diatonic or chromatic using definition 1:

1. Determine the key of the composition, and which notes receive sharps or flats.
2. If the half-step is part of the major or minor scale upon which the music is based, including half-steps that occur in the harmonic or melodic forms of minor, it is diatonic.
3. If the half-step is not within the key, it is chromatic.

Example:

1. Key of g minor.
2. Half-step **A**, F♯ to G, is in the g harmonic minor scale. The half-step is diatonic.
3. Half-step **B**, G♯ to A, is not in any form of the g minor scale. The half-step is chromatic.

Beethoven: *Sonata, Op. 49, No. 1*

Definition 2: Diatonic half-steps are formed by notes with two different letter names. (Using this definition, half-steps **A** and **B** are diatonic.)

Both definitions: Chromatic half-steps are formed by notes with the same letter name.

3. Name the key for each of the following phrases. Mark whether each circled half step is diatonic or chromatic, using both definitions.

a. From *Sinfonia No. 9* by J.S. Bach. Key of: _____ _____

Definition 1: ___ ___ ___ ___ ___ ___ ___

Definition 2: ___ ___ ___ ___ ___ ___ ___

b. From *Sonata (Erstveroffentlichung),* by Haydn. Key of: _____ _____

Definition 1: ___ ___ ___ ___ ___ ___

Definition 2: ___ ___ ___ ___ ___ ___

c. From *French Suite No. 1: Menuet,* by J.S. Bach. Key of: _____ _____

Definition 1: _____ _____ _____ _____

Definition 2: _____ _____ _____ _____

d. From *Sonata, XVI:40,* by Haydn. Key of: _____ _____

Definition 1: _____ _____ _____ _____ _____

Definition 2: _____ _____ _____ _____ _____

LESSON 5
MAJOR, MINOR AUGMENTED AND DIMINISHED TRIADS AND INVERSIONS

A **TRIAD** is a three-note chord, based on the interval of a third.

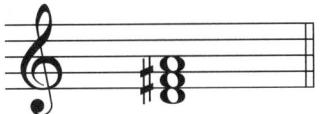

D Major Triad

MAJOR TRIADS are formed by of the first, third, and fifth notes of the Major scale with the same name. The lowest note of a Major triad in root position names the triad. The three notes are called **ROOT**, **THIRD**, and **FIFTH**.

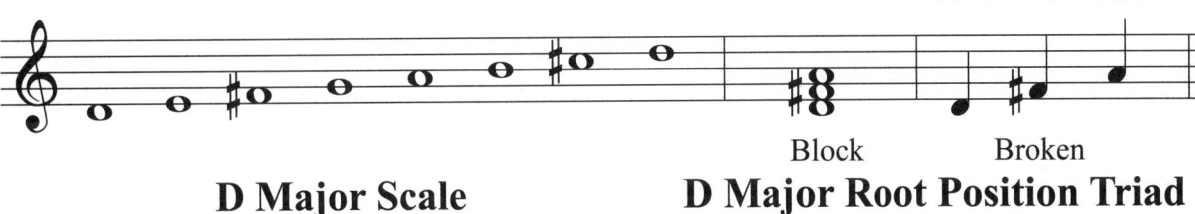

D Major Scale   **D Major Root Position Triad**

To change a Major triad into a **MINOR** triad, lower third a half-step. Minor triads have the same sharps or flats as the minor key signature with the same name.

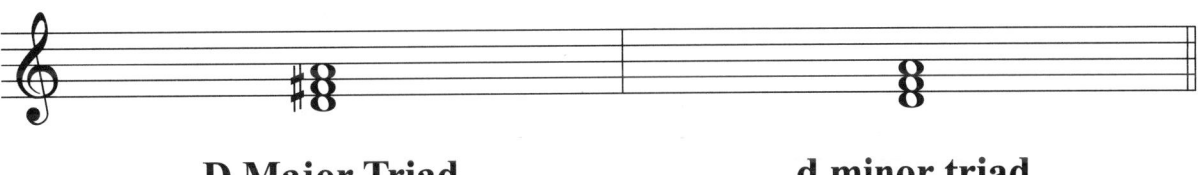

D Major Triad   **d minor triad**

29

To change a Major triad into an **AUGMENTED** triad, raise the fifth a half-step. The intervals between the root and third and between the third and fifth are Major 3rds.

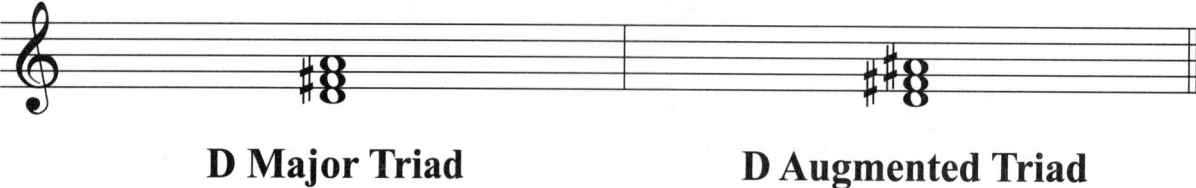

To change a Major triad into a **DIMINISHED** triad, lower both the third and the fifth a half-step. The intervals between the root and third and between the third and fifth are minor 3rds.

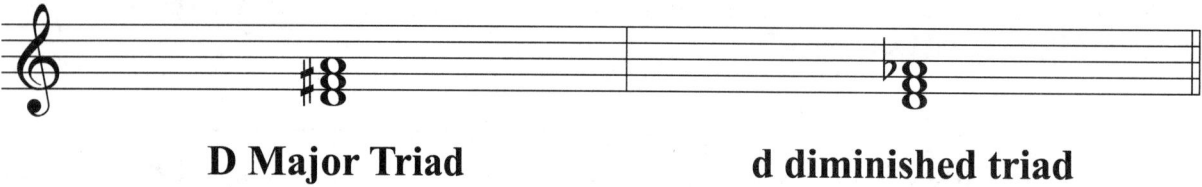

A **ROOT POSITION TRIAD** occurs when the root is the lowest note. **FIGURED BASS** is used to indicate the position or inversion. The figured bass for root position is $\frac{5}{3}$, because when the triad is in its simplest position, the intervals above the root create a fifth and a third. When labeling a triad in root position, only the letter name and quality are needed. Figured bass is optional.

D Major Root Position Triad
D Major or D Major $\frac{5}{3}$

A **FIRST INVERSION TRIAD** occurs when the **third** is the lowest note. The figured bass for first inversion is $^6_3$, because the intervals that are formed by the notes are a 6th and a 3rd.

When labeling first inversion triads, the symbol ^{6} or $^6_3$ is written to the right of the name.

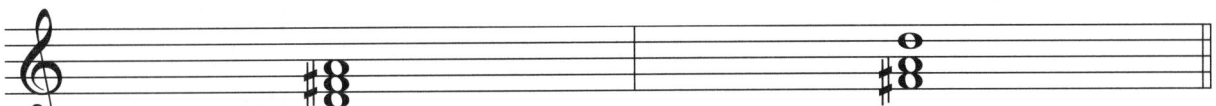

D Major Root Position Triad
D Major or D Major $^5_3$

D Major First Inversion Triad
D Major ^{6} or D Major $^6_3$

A **SECOND INVERSION TRIAD** occurs when the **fifth** is the lowest note. The figured bass for second inversion is $^6_4$, because when the triads are in their simplest position they include the intervals of a 6th and a 4th.

When labeling second inversion triads, the symbol $^6_4$ is written after the name of the triad.

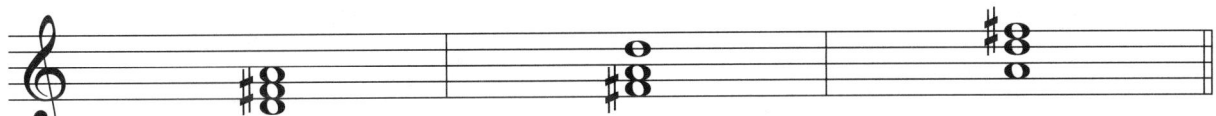

D Major
Root Position Triad
D Major
or D Major $^5_3$

D Major
First Inversion Triad
D Major ^{6}
or D Major $^6_3$

D Major
Second Inversion Triad
D Major $^6_4$

1. Notate each of the following triads in root position, first inversion, and second inversion.

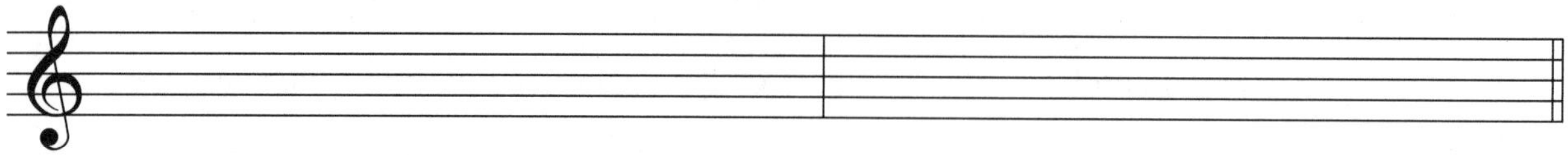

A♭ Major | c minor

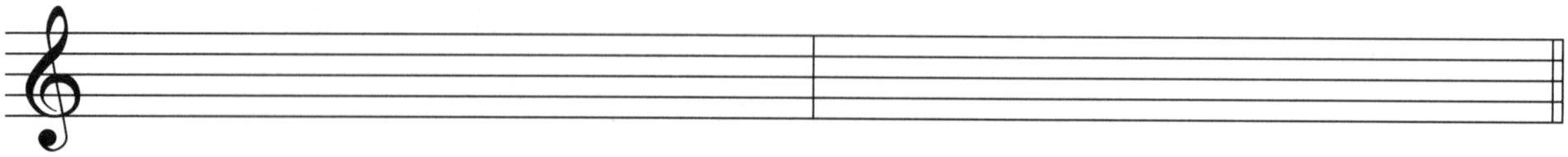

G Major | e♭ diminished

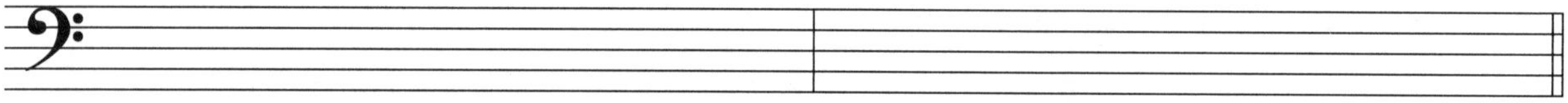

E Augmented | b♭ diminished

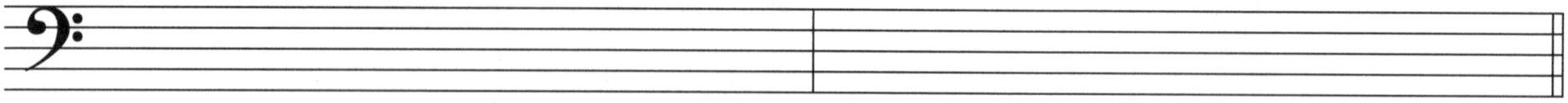

A Augmented | d diminished

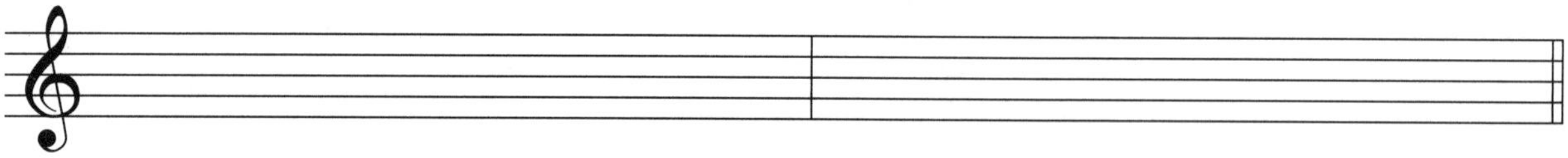

c♯ minor | F Major

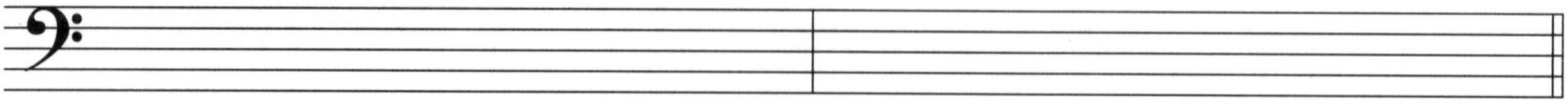

F♯ Augmented | B Major

2. Name each of the following triads with its root, quality, and figured bass.

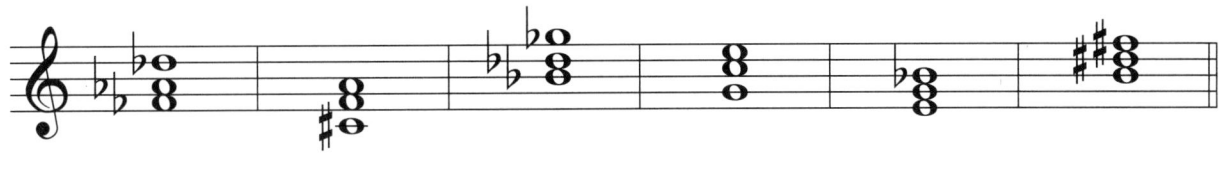

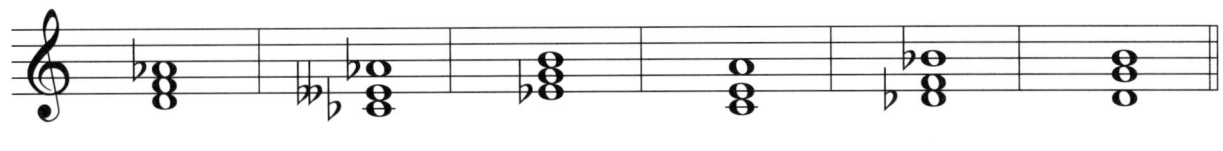

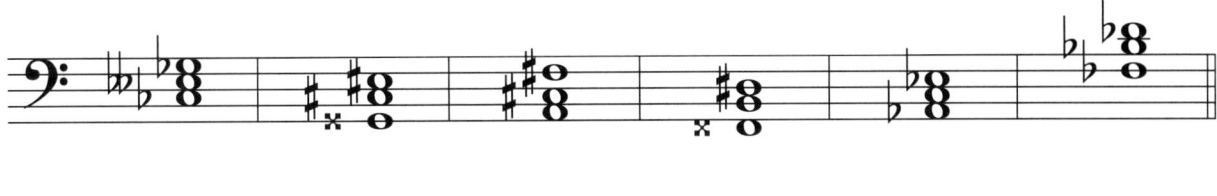

3. Notate each of the following triads.

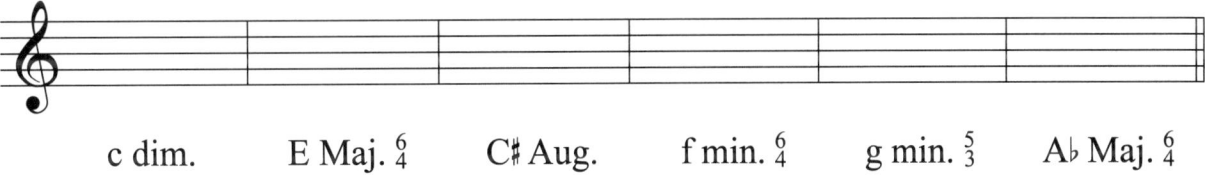

c dim.   E Maj. $^6_4$ C♯ Aug.   f min. $^6_4$ g min. $^5_3$ A♭ Maj. $^6_4$

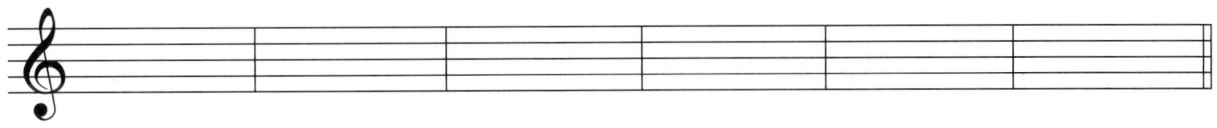

B Aug. ^{6} d dim. $^6_3$ f♯ dim. $^5_3$ B♭ Maj. $^6_4$ E♭ Aug. $^6_4$ a min.

F Maj. ^{6} C Maj. $^6_4$ c♯ min. $^6_3$ e min. ^{6} D Aug. $^5_3$ e♭ dim. $^6_3$

In actual music, triads are rarely in their simplest positions. To determine the root and quality of a triad within a composition, follow these steps:

a. Put the triad in its simplest form by placing the note names so that there is one letter between each (for example, F-C-F-A becomes F-A-C), or draw the root position triad on a staff.

b. Add all sharps or flats from the key signature or from earlier in the measure to the notes.

c. Determine the root and quality of the triad.

d. Determine the inversion of the triad by looking at the lowest note on the <u>lowest</u> staff.

Example (From *Minuet in G* by Beethoven):

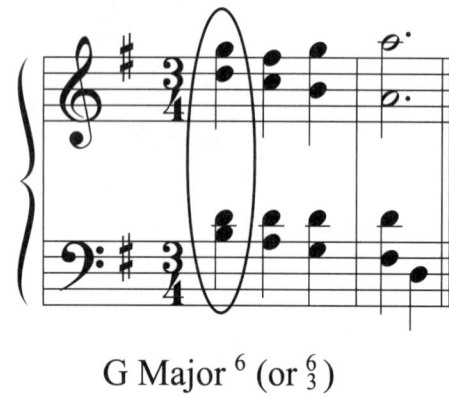

G Major ^{6} (or $^6_3$)

a. Notes are B-D-D-G.

b. Simplest form is G-B-D.

c. G Major Triad.

d. B is the lowest note (in the bass clef), so the triad is in first inversion ($^6_3$).

e. G Major ^{6} (or G Major $^6_3$)

If only two notes are present in the chord they will most likely be the root and third, with the root doubled.

4. Name each of the following boxed triads with its root, quality, and figured bass.

a. From *Sonata, Op. 14, No. 1,* by Beethoven.

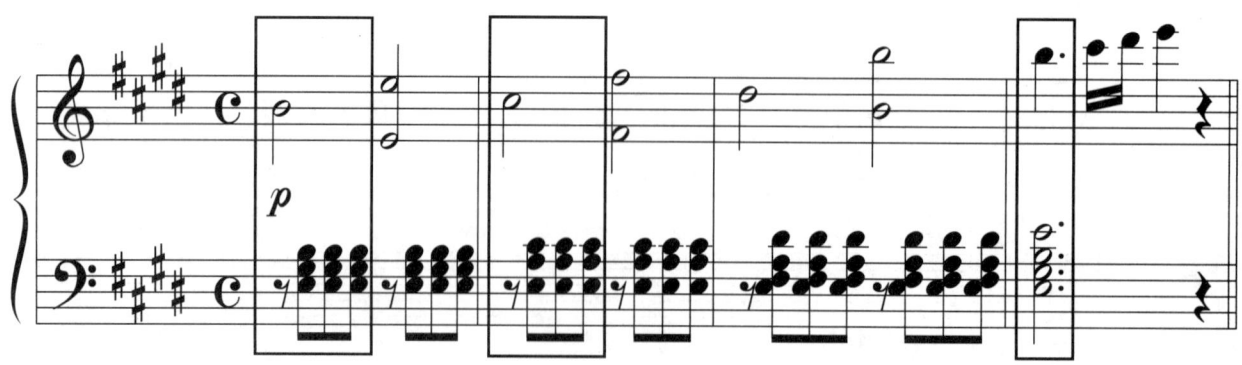

_____   _____   _____

b. From *Rhapsody, Op. 119, No. 4,* by Brahms.

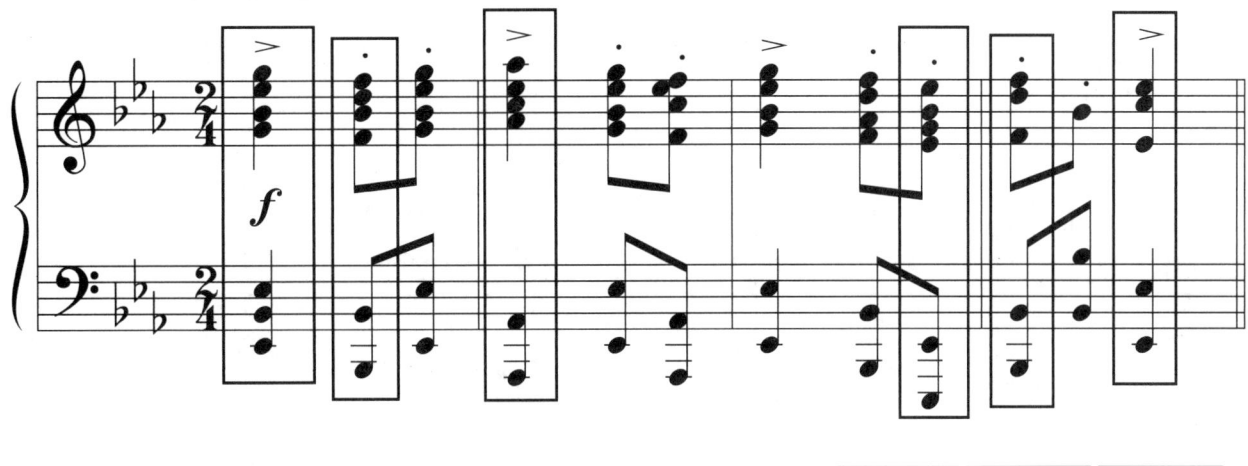

c. From *French Suite No. 1: Menuet,* by J.S. Bach.

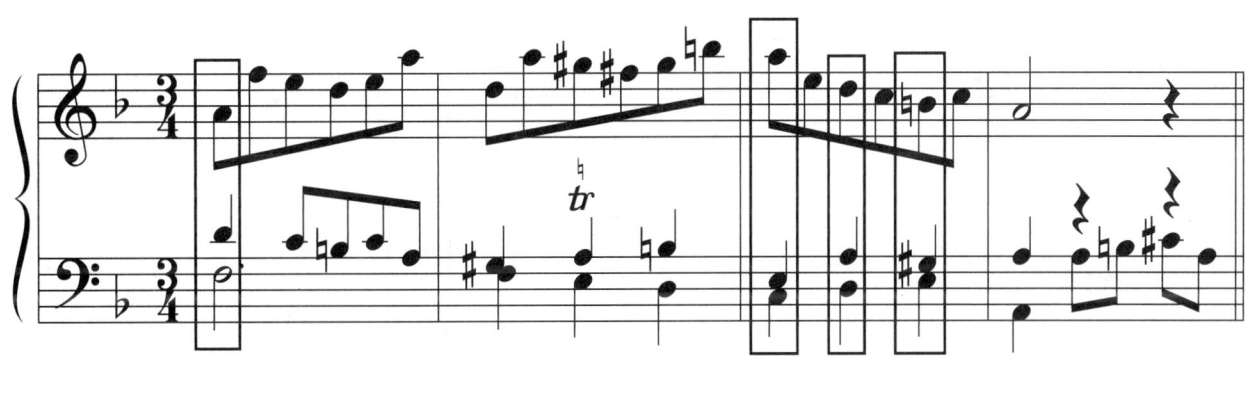

d. From *Sonata No. 32* by Scarlatti.

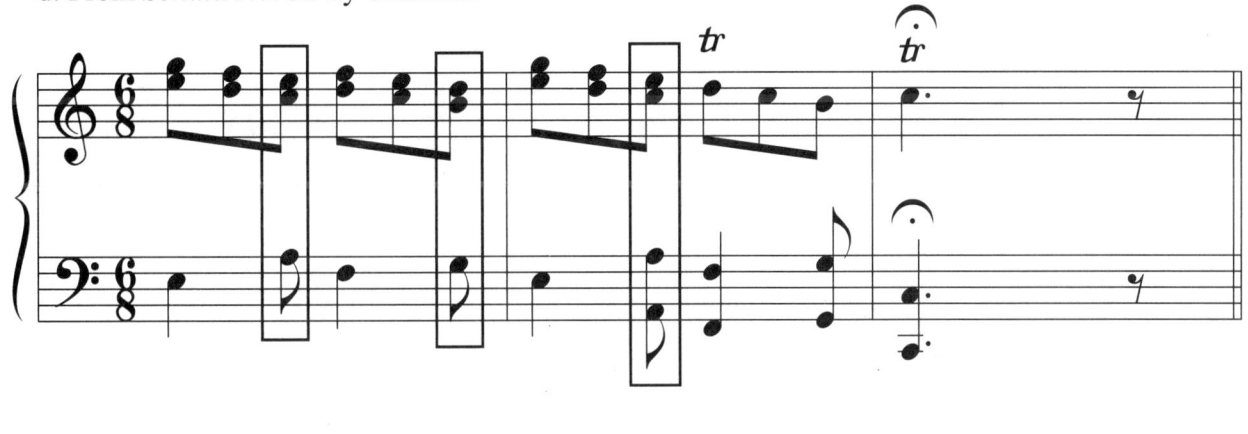

e. From *Aufschwung* by Schumann.

f. From *Sonata, K. 280,* by Mozart.

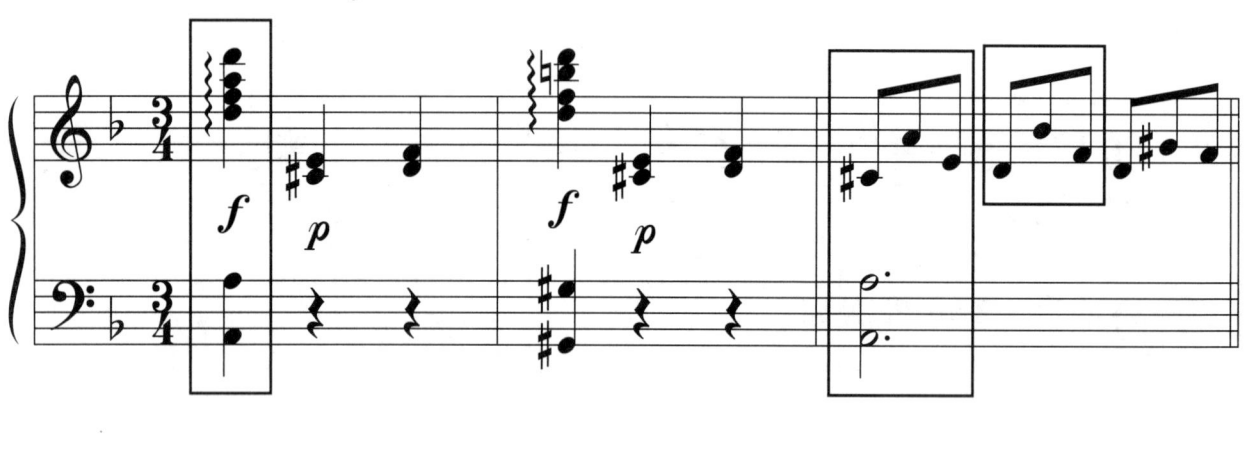

g. From *Sonata, K. 283,* by Mozart.

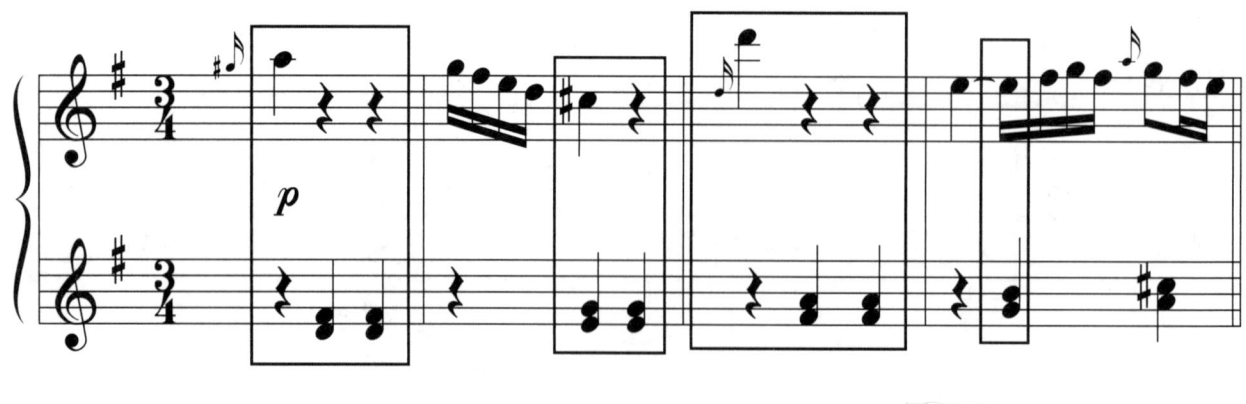

LESSON 6
PRIMARY AND SECONDARY TRIADS

A triad can be built on each note of the scale.

When building triads on scale tones, all of the sharps or flats that are in the key are added to the chords which have those notes.

Example: D Major Scale has F♯ and C♯. When writing the triads of D Major, every time an F or C appears in a chord, a sharp must be added to it.

Triads of the scale are numbered using Roman numerals. Upper case Roman numerals are used for Major triads, lower case Roman numerals are used for minor triads, upper case Roman numerals with "+" are used for Augmented triads, and lower case Roman numerals with "○" are used for diminished triads.

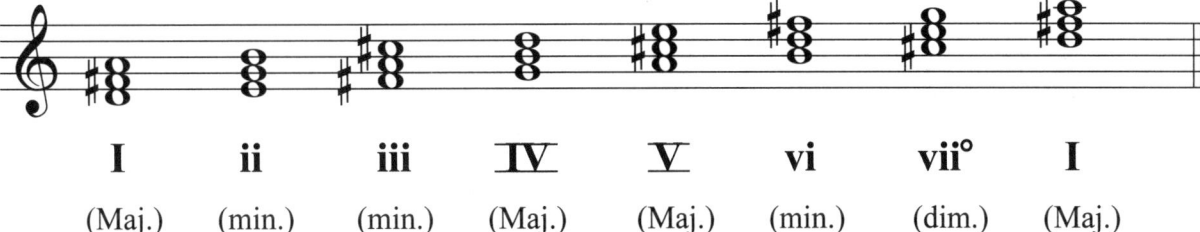

PRIMARY AND SECONDARY TRIADS IN THE KEY OF D MAJOR

I, IV, and V are the **PRIMARY TRIADS**. In Major keys, these three triads are Major, and are the most commonly used chords for harmonizing tonal melodies. The chords are labeled with upper case Roman numerals.

ii, iii, vi, and vii° are the **SECONDARY TRIADS**. In Major keys, ii, iii, and vi are minor, and vii° is diminished. The chords are labeled with lower case Roman numerals, and the vii° chord has a small circle beside the Roman numeral.

The qualities of the triads in minor keys are different from those for Major keys. When using **harmonic minor**, the triads have the following qualities:

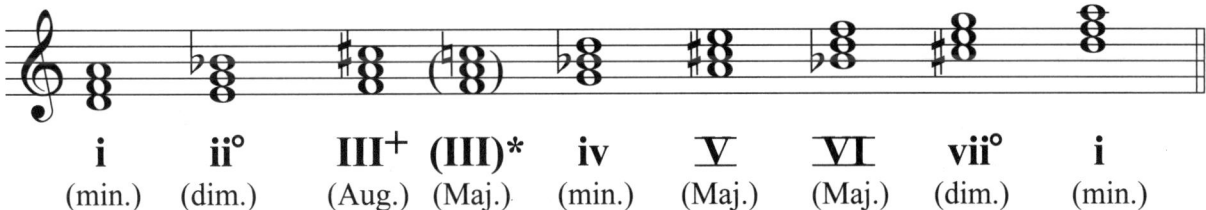

PRIMARY AND SECONDARY TRIADS IN THE KEY OF D MINOR

*Typically, the Augmented III (III⁺) chord is not used in minor keys. The III chord is usually Major, and is often found when the key is moving to the relative Major.

The triads of the whole tone scale all sound augmented, but the triads should be written using the scale tones, not as root position triads. There are only six different chords, since there are only six different notes in the scale.

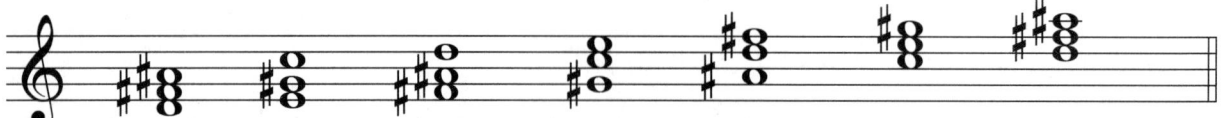

TRIADS OF THE WHOLE TONE SCALE ON D

1. Notate the primary and secondary triads for each of the following keys and label the triads with Roman numerals. Circle each primary triad and put a box around each secondary triad. Do not use a key signature. Draw sharps or flats before the notes. The first one is given.

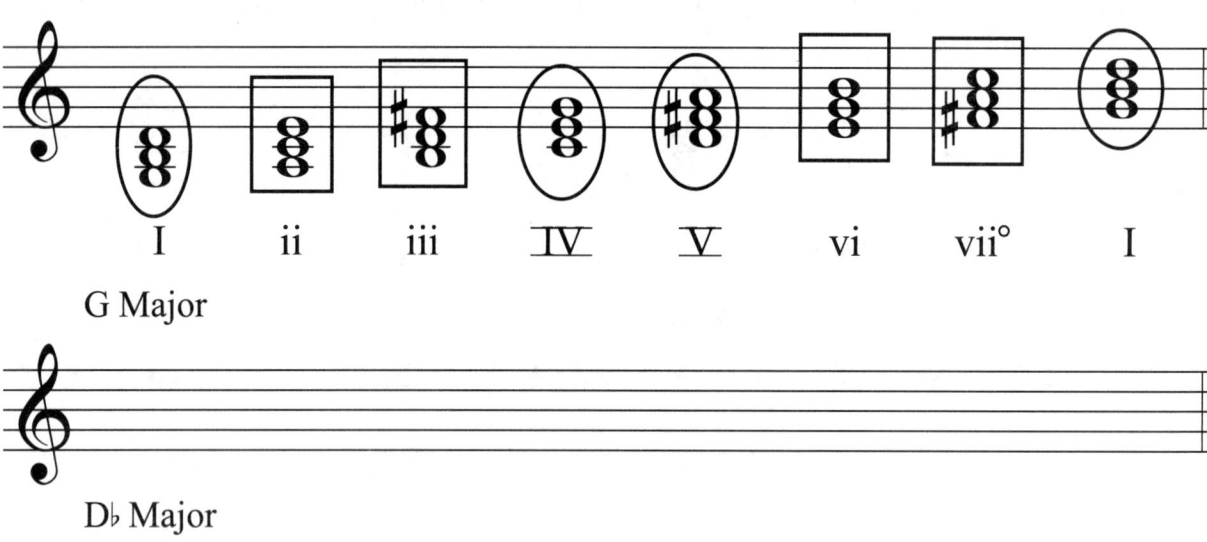

G Major

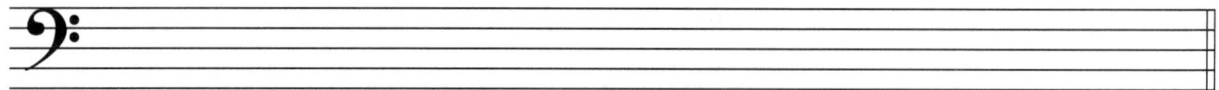

D♭ Major

Whole Tone on A (Do not circle chords or write Roman numerals)

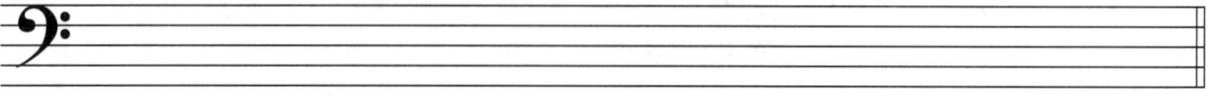

B♭ Major

2. Notate the primary triads for each of the following keys and label the triads with Roman numerals. Do not use a key signature. Draw sharps or flats before the notes. The first one is given.

    I   IV   V

C Major   D Major

E♭ Major   e minor

f minor   F♯ Major

c♯ minor   A♭ Major

e♭ minor   A Major

G Major   B♭ Major

3. Notate the Secondary Triads for each of the following keys and label the triads with Roman numerals. Do not use a key signature. Draw sharps or flats before the notes. The first one is given.

Each degree of the scale has a name. These are called the **SCALE DEGREE NAMES:**

The **I** chord is **TONIC**.

The **ii** chord is **SUPERTONIC**.

The **iii** chord is **MEDIANT**.

The **IV** chord is **SUBDOMINANT**.

The **V** chord is **DOMINANT**.

The **vi** chord is **SUBMEDIANT**.

The **vii°** chord is **LEADING TONE**.

(Note: Qualities used above are from Major keys. The names stay the same when in minor.)

4. Match each of the following Roman numerals with its scale degree names.

a. ii   _____ Submediant

b. I   _____ Dominant

c. iii   _____ Supertonic

d. vii°   _____ Subdominant

e. IV   _____ Leading Tone

f. vi   _____ Mediant

g. V   _____ Tonic

5. Write the scale degree names for each of the following Roman numerals.

I _____

ii _____

iii _____

IV _____

V _____

vi _____

vii° _____

In actual music, chords are rarely in their simplest position. To determine the Roman numeral of a chord within a composition, follow these steps:

a. Determine the Major or minor key of the music.

b. Name the chord with its root and quality.

c. Determine the Roman numeral of the chord by counting from the name of the key up to the name of the chord.

d. Determine the inversion of the chord by looking at the lowest note (on the <u>lowest</u> staff).

Example (From *Minuet in G* by Beethoven):

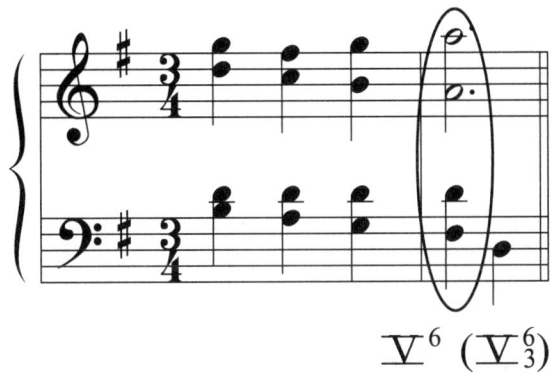

$\underline{V}^6$ ($\underline{V}^6_3$)

a. Key of G Major

b. D Major triad

c. D is the fifth note of the G Major Scale; therefore, this is the $\underline{V}$ chord.

d. The lowest note (in the bass clef) is F♯. The chord is in first inversion.

e. $\underline{V}^6_3$ or $\underline{V}^6$

Tips:

1. Be sure to determine whether the music is in the Major key or the minor key.

2. Use upper-case and lower-case Roman numerals correctly.

3. Draw lines above and below Roman numerals for Major triads. This is to differentiate between the qualities when the Roman numeral is hand-written. (When Roman numerals are computer-generated, the distinction between capital and lower-case letters is obvious, so the lines are not necessary.)

4. Look for accidentals that appear earlier in the measure.

5. If the Roman numerals are unusual, such as a Major VII chord, you may be using the wrong key. Double-check your key signature.

6. For each of the following phrases, name the key and label the boxed chords with Roman numerals and figured bass.

a. From *Sonata, K. 284,* by Mozart. Key of: _____ _____

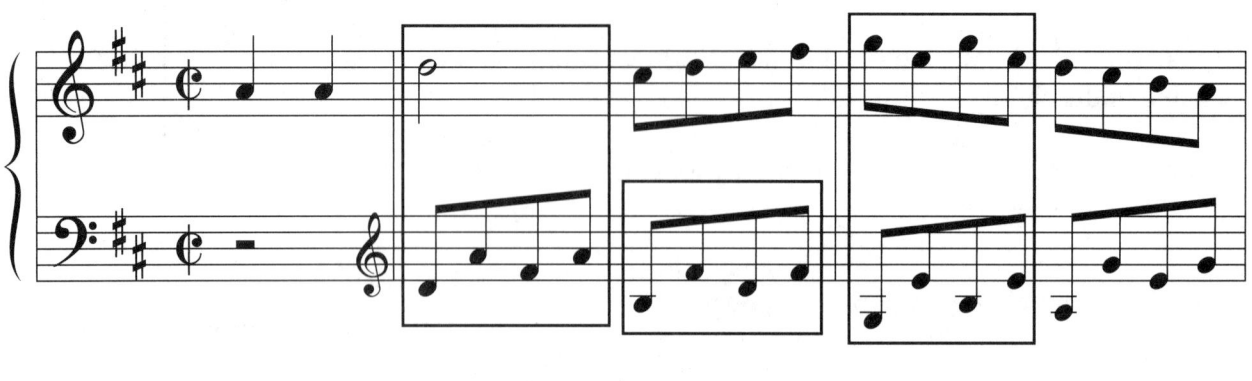

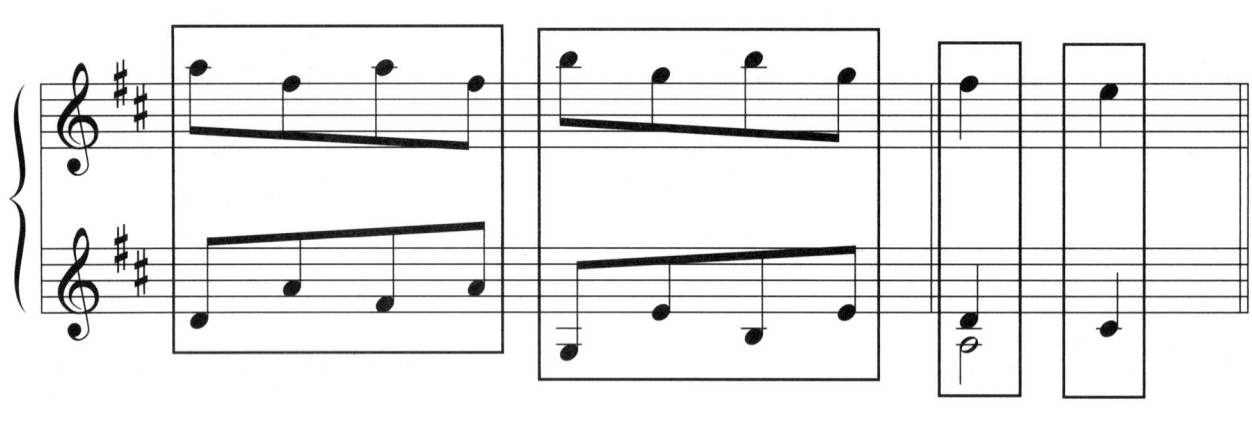

b. From *Sonata No. 40* by Scarlatti. Key of: _____ _____

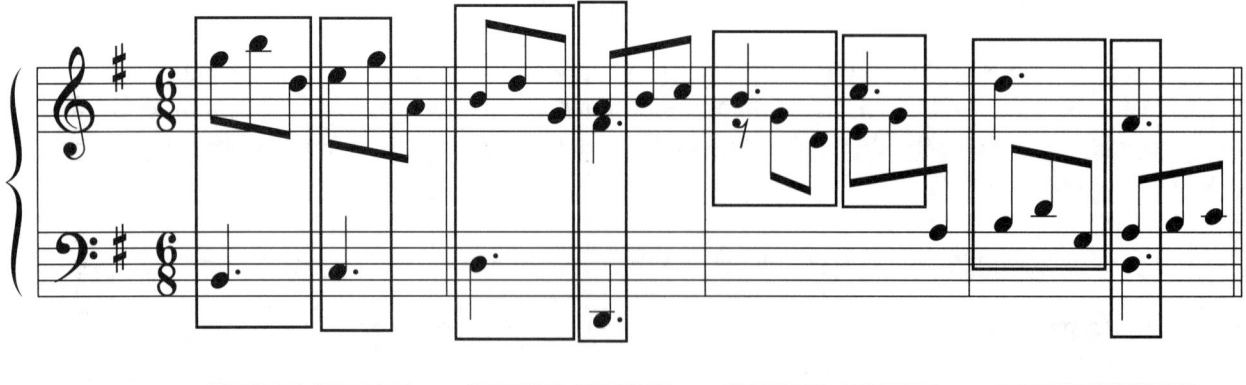

c. From *Grillen* by Schumann. Key of: _____ _____

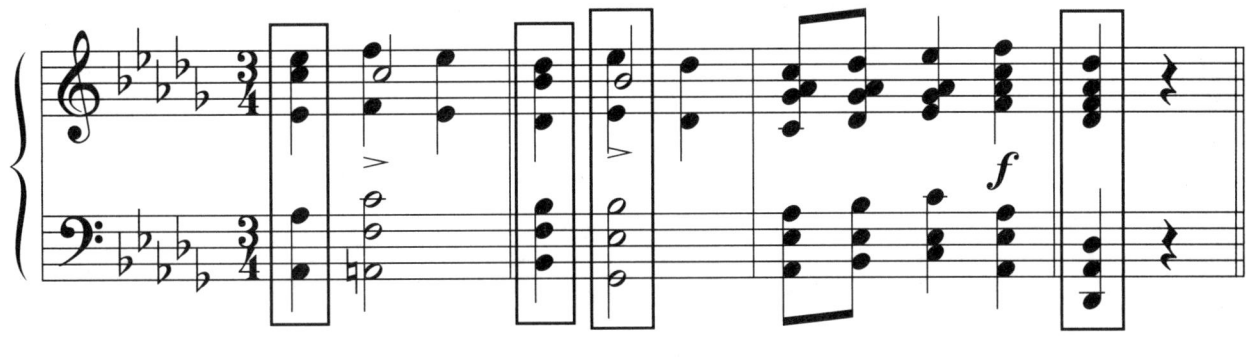

d. From *French Suite No. 3: Menuet II,* by J.S. Bach. Key of: _____ _____

e. From *Sonata, K. 281,* by Mozart. Key of: _____ _____

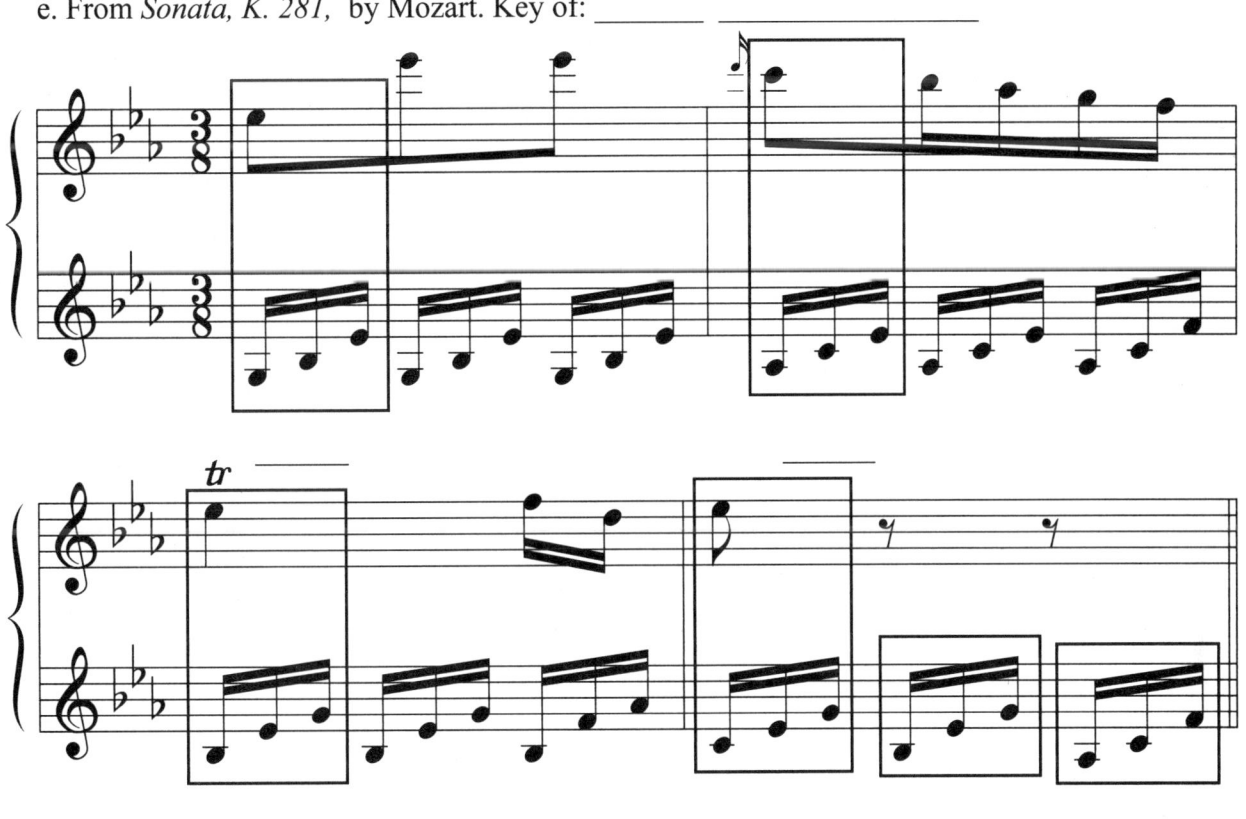

f. From *Sonata, Hob. XVI:42,* by Haydn. Key of: _____ _____

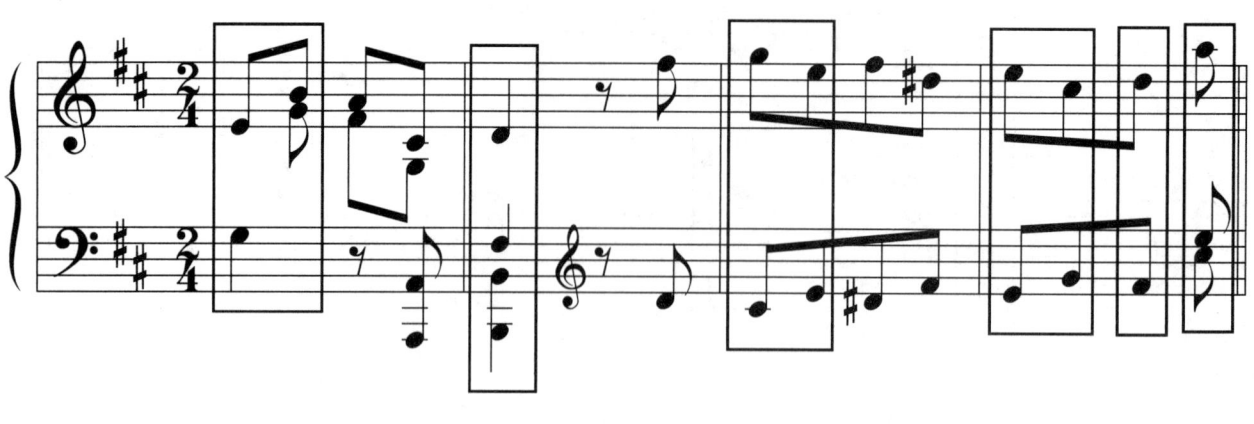

LESSON 7
SEVENTH CHORDS

SEVENTH CHORDS are chords which contain four different notes, and are made up of a triad plus the interval of 7th above the root.

The **DOMINANT SEVENTH CHORD** is created when a fourth note is added to the V chord (the Dominant chord). This fourth note is a seventh above the root of the chord. The chord consists of a Major triad on the bottom, with the added interval of a minor 7th.

The chord is named Dominant 7th because it is based on the V or Dominant chord, and has the interval of a 7th within the chord.

Inversions of the Dominant seventh chord are:

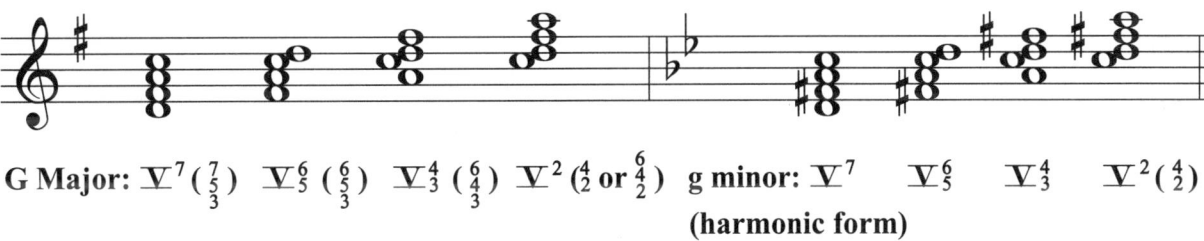

Dominant seventh chords can be on a note, or in a key. When asked to write a Dominant seventh on a given note, write a Major triad and add a minor 7th above the root.

When asked to write a Dominant seventh in a given key, find the V chord for that key, and add a note which is a minor seventh above the root. In Major keys, no accidentals will be added to the chord. In minor keys, the third will be raised because of harmonic minor.

1. Notate Dominant seventh chords and their inversions in each of the following keys. Label the chords with Roman numerals and figured bass. Use the harmonic form of minor.

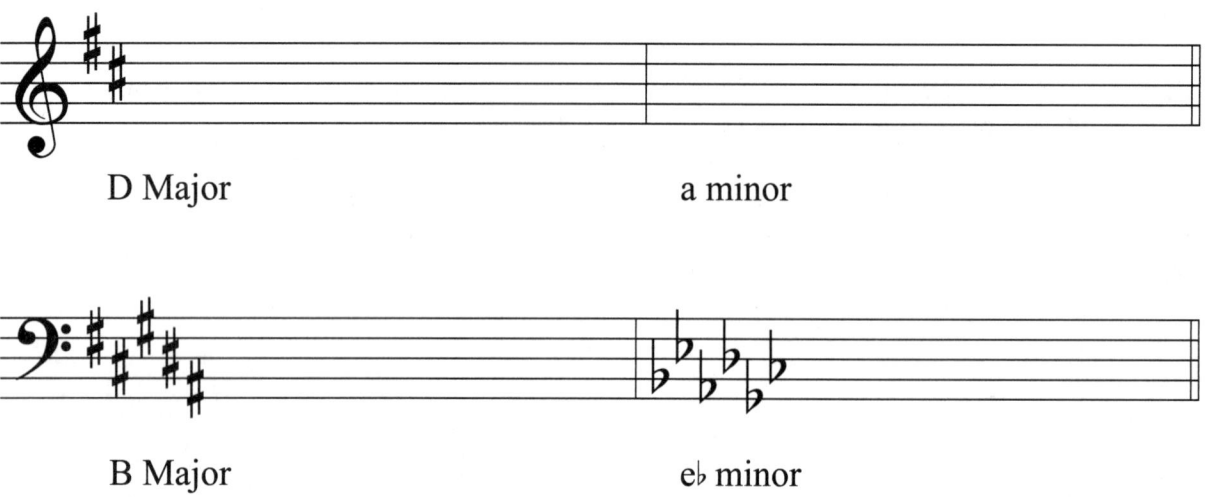

D Major   a minor

B Major   e♭ minor

2. Complete Dominant seventh chords and their inversions on each of the following roots.

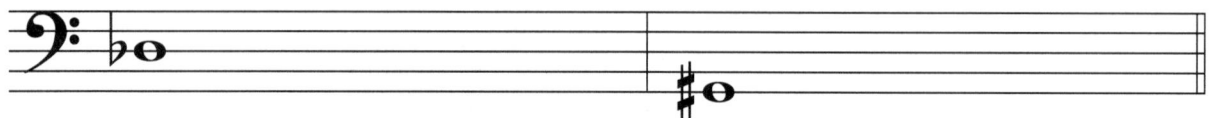

MAJOR SEVENTH CHORDS consist of a Major triad and a Major 7th above the root. When writing Major seventh chords, all sharps or flats from the Major key signature of the root will be included.

D Major Triad   Major 7th   D Major
                              Seventh Chord

MAJOR SEVENTH CHORD ON D

3. Notate the following Major seventh chords and their inversions.

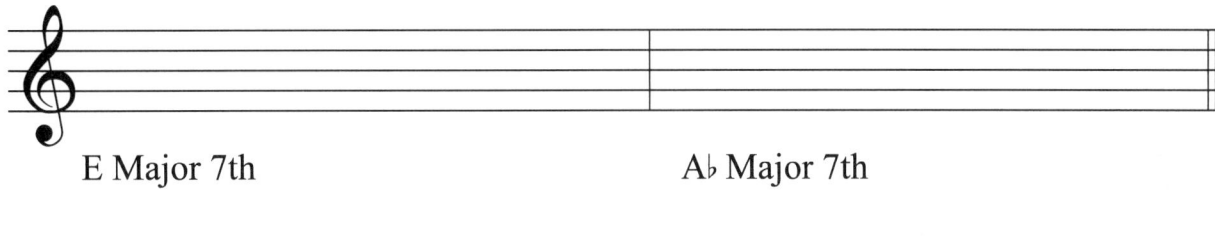

E Major 7th   A♭ Major 7th

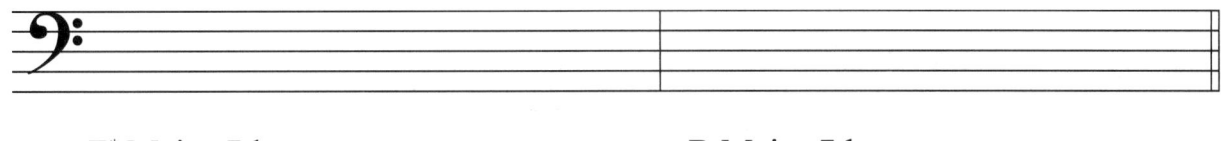

F♯ Major 7th   B Major 7th

MINOR SEVENTH CHORDS contain a minor triad and the interval of a minor seventh above the root. When writing minor seventh chords, all sharps or flats from the minor key signature of the root (natural form) will be included.

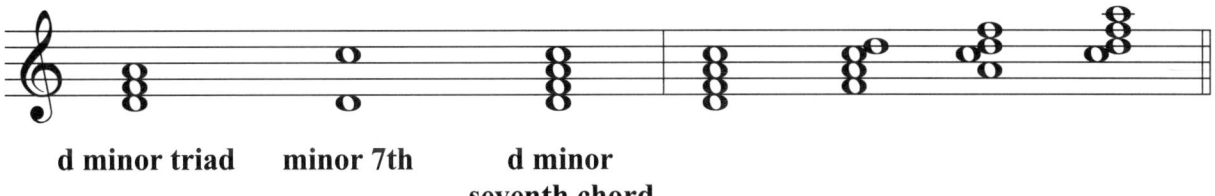

d minor triad   minor 7th   d minor seventh chord

MINOR SEVENTH CHORD ON D

4. Notate the following minor seventh chords and their inversions.

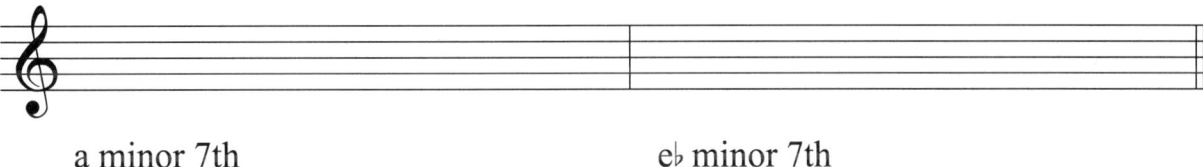

a minor 7th   e♭ minor 7th

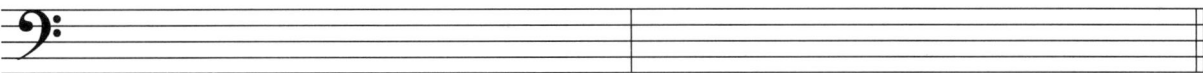

b minor 7th   c minor 7th

HALF-DIMINISHED SEVENTH CHORDS consist of a diminished triad plus a minor seventh above the root.

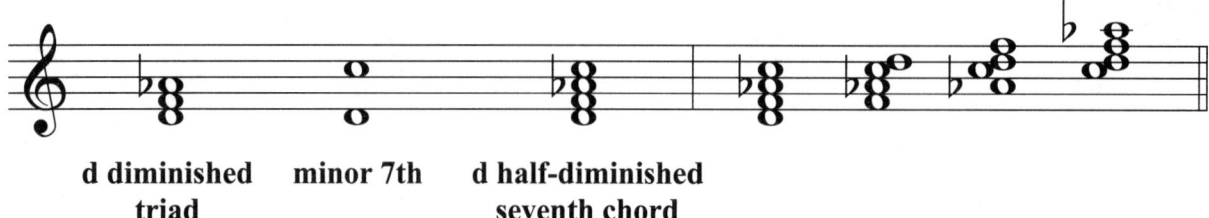

d diminished triad   minor 7th   d half-diminished seventh chord

HALF-DIMINISHED SEVENTH CHORD ON D
($d^{ø7}$)

5. Notate the following half-diminished seventh chords and their inversions.

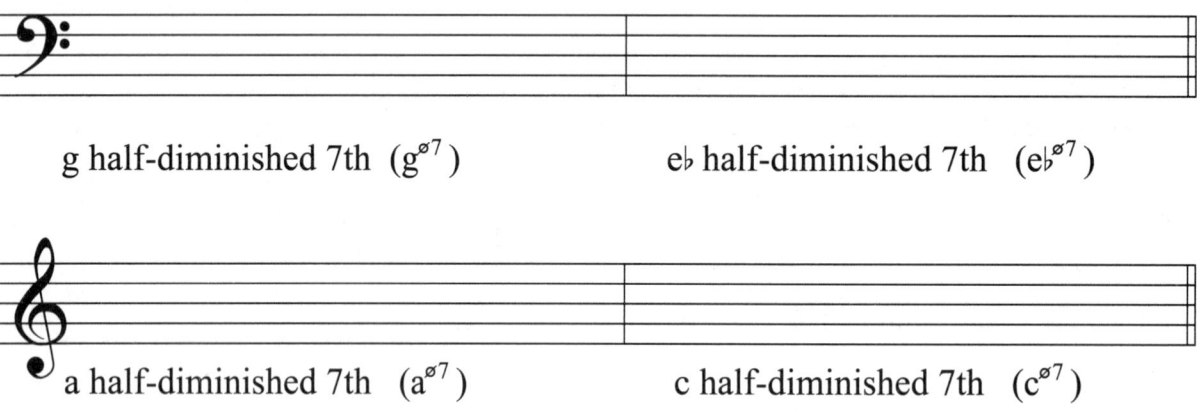

g half-diminished 7th ($g^{ø7}$)   e♭ half-diminished 7th ($e♭^{ø7}$)

a half-diminished 7th ($a^{ø7}$)   c half-diminished 7th ($c^{ø7}$)

DIMINISHED SEVENTH CHORDS consist of a diminished triad plus the interval of a diminished seventh above the root.

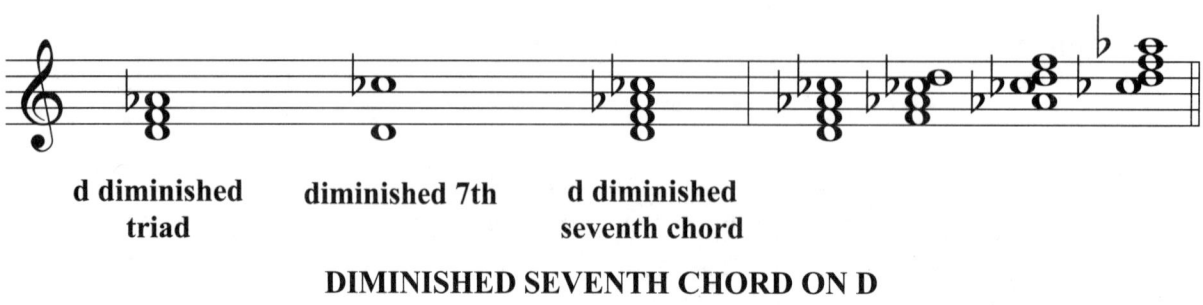

d diminished triad   diminished 7th   d diminished seventh chord

DIMINISHED SEVENTH CHORD ON D
($d^{°7}$)

6. Notate the following diminished 7th chords and their inversions.

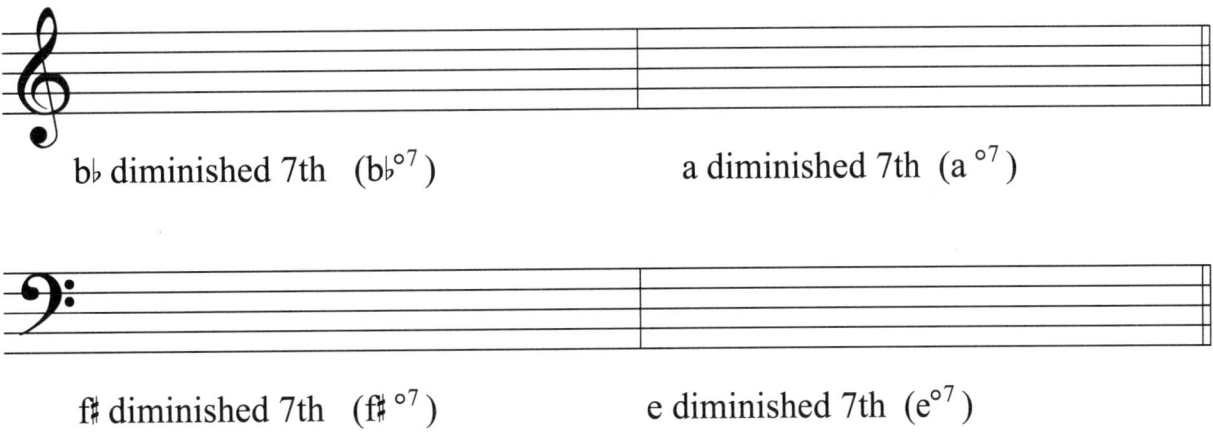

b♭ diminished 7th (b♭°7)   a diminished 7th (a°7)

f♯ diminished 7th (f♯°7)   e diminished 7th (e°7)

7. Label each of the following seventh chords with its root, quality, and figured bass.

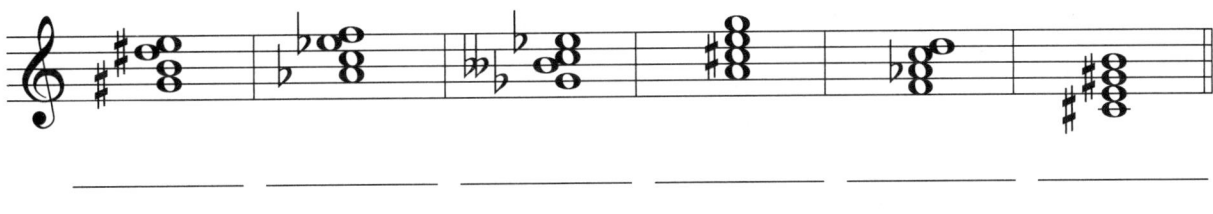

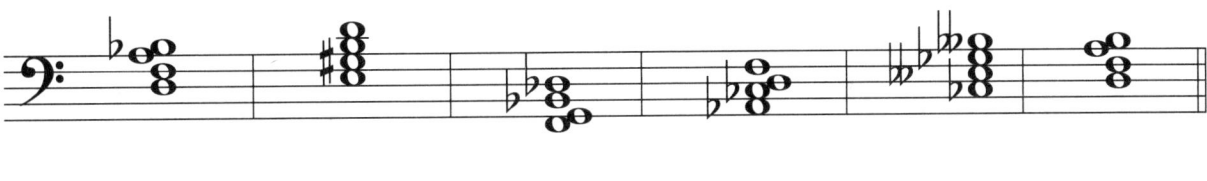

8. Label each boxed chord with its root, quality, and figured bass. The first one is given.

a. From *Invention No. 14* by J.S. Bach.

B♭ Dominant $\frac{4}{3}$

b. From *Nocturne, Op. posth. 72, No. 1,* by Chopin.

c. From *Rhapsody, Op. 119, No. 4,* by Brahms.

d. From *Sonata, Hob. XVI:34,* by Haydn.

i. From *Grillen* by Schumann.

j. Anonymous

k. From *French Suite No. 3: Menuet II,* by J.S. Bach.

l. Anonymous.

LESSON 8
THE SECONDARY DOMINANT

Frequently, chords appear that are not within the key of the composition. One of these is the **SECONDARY DOMINANT**. Secondary dominants add color and variety to the music.

The secondary dominant is the Dominant (V) or Dominant seventh (V^7) of a key other than tonic (I). It usually resolves to the chord which would be tonic of the key to which it belongs.

Secondary dominants include accidentals that are not in the key signature, and their qualities are different from those of the primary and secondary triads.

Examples in the key of C Major:

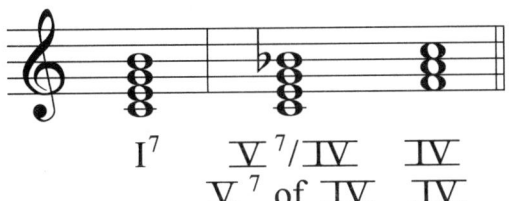

(I^7 chord does not have a flatted or minor 7th. $V7$ of IV has a Dominant seventh quality.)

I⁷   V⁷/IV   IV
     V⁷ of IV   IV

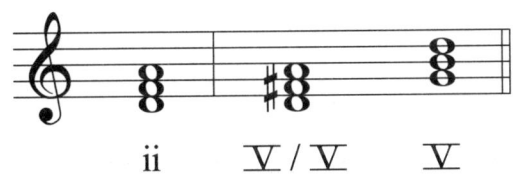

(ii chord is minor; V of V is Major.)

ii   V/V   V
     V of V   V

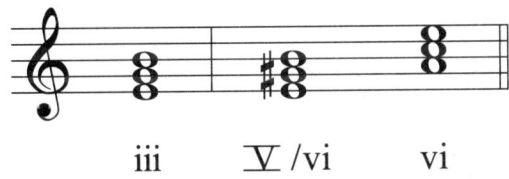

(iii chord is minor; V of vi is Major.)

iii   V/vi   vi
      V of vi   vi

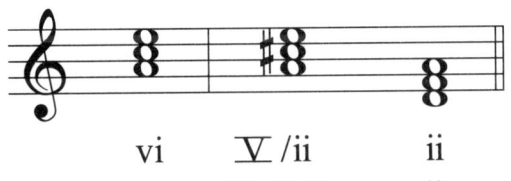

(vi chord is minor; V of ii is Major.)

vi   V/ii   ii
     V of ii   ii

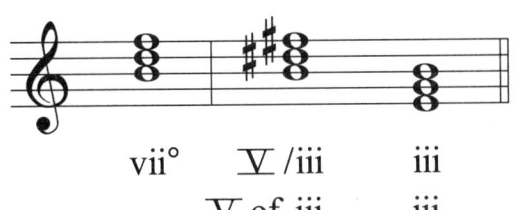

vii° chord is diminished; V of iii is Major.)

vii°   V/iii   iii
       V of iii   iii

To notate secondary dominants and their resolutions:

1. Find and notate the <u>second</u> chord (the resolution).

A Major: V^6_5/iii iii

2. Find the V or V^7 chord of the resolution. The root of the secondary dominant will be same note as the fifth of the resolution. Notate the Major or Dominant 7th chord in root position.

A Major: V^7/iii iii

3. Put the chords into the correct positions.

A Major: V^6_5/iii iii

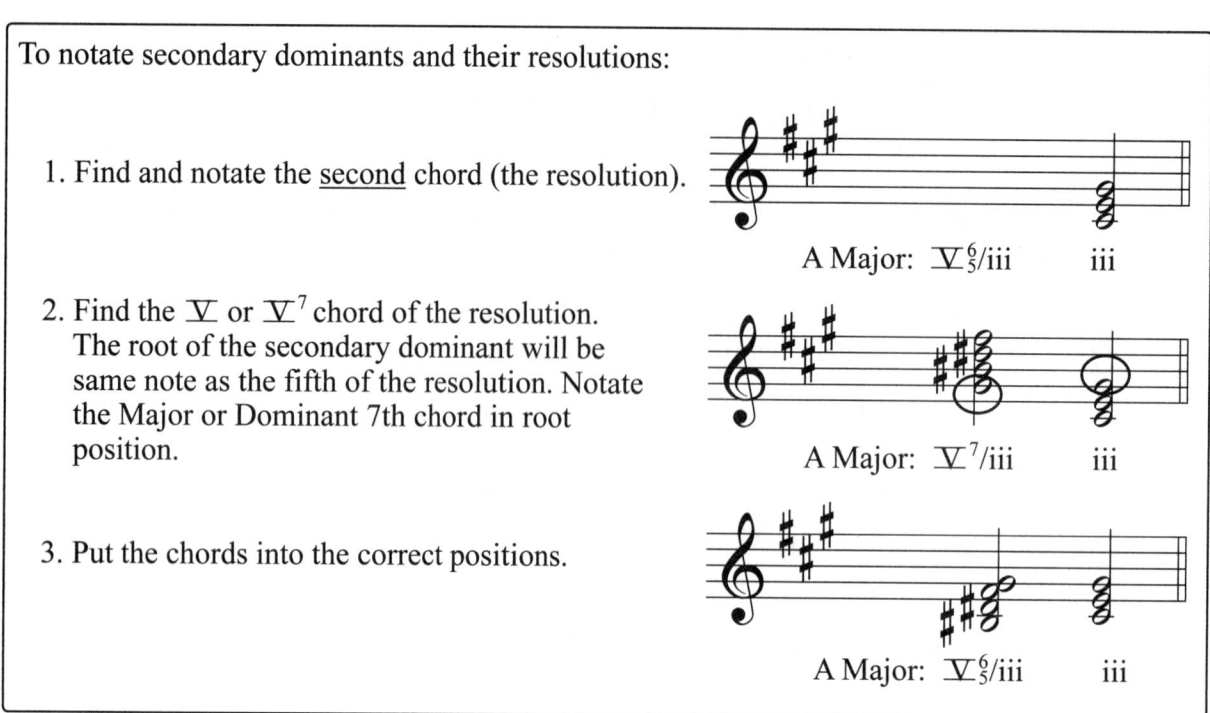

1. Notate each of the following secondary dominants and its resolution. Determine whether to use the Major or minor key by the quality of the second Roman numeral except where indicated. Use the harmonic form for minor keys. V^7/___ is the same as V^7 of ___.

V of iii iii^6_4 | V^7 of V V^6_4 (Major) | V^4_3 of vi vi^6 | V^6 of V V (Major)

V^6_5/ ii ii | V^2/ ii ii^6 | V^6_4 / iv iv^6 | V / vi vi^6_4

V^6_5 of V V (minor) | V^6_3 of VI VI | V^7 of iii iii^6_4 | V of iii iii^6_4

V^6_5/IV IV | V^2/ ii ii^6 | V^4_3/V V^6 (minor) | V^7/IV IV^6_4

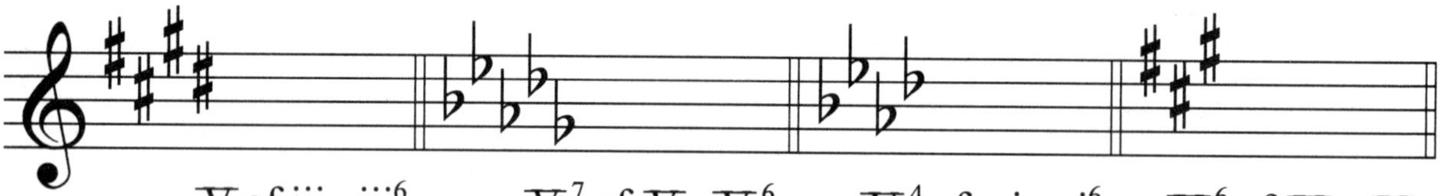

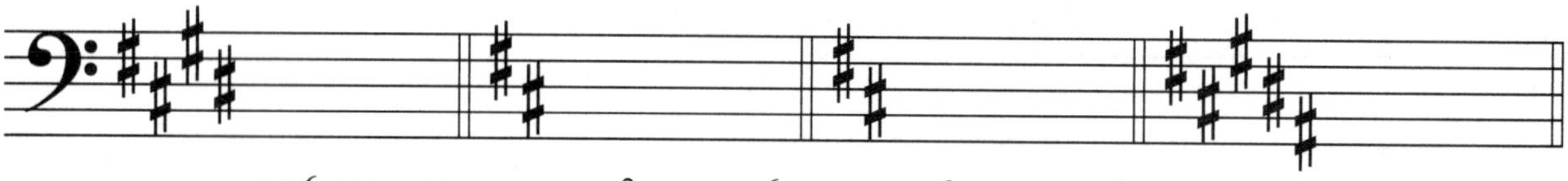

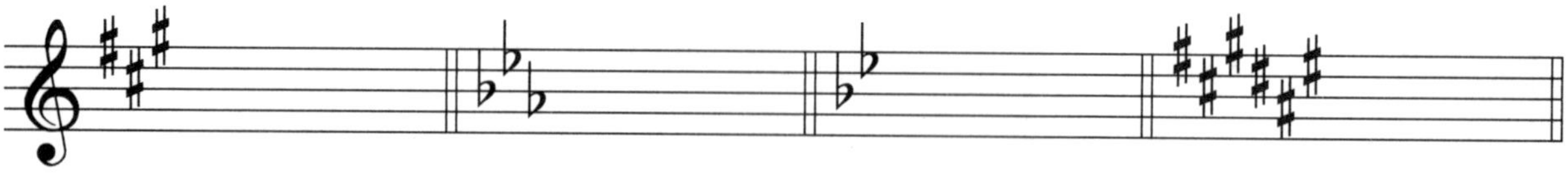

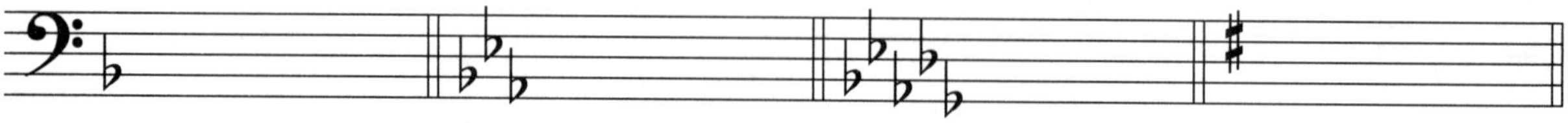

To label secondary dominants in a composition:

1. Determine the key.

2. Label the second chord (the resolution) with its Roman numeral and figured bass.

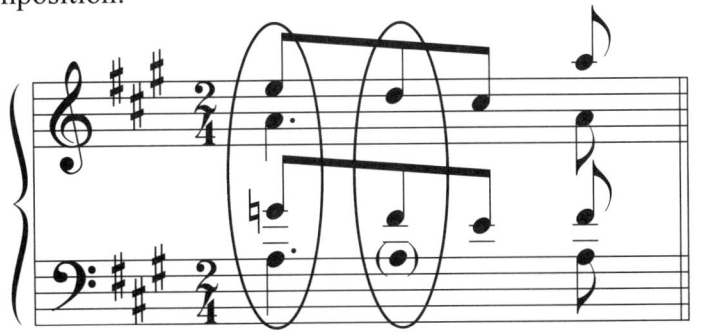

A Major: ____ / ____ IV$^6_4$

3. The Roman numeral for the second half of the secondary dominant will be the same as the resolution. Write the Roman numeral for the resolution after the /. Do not include the figured bass.

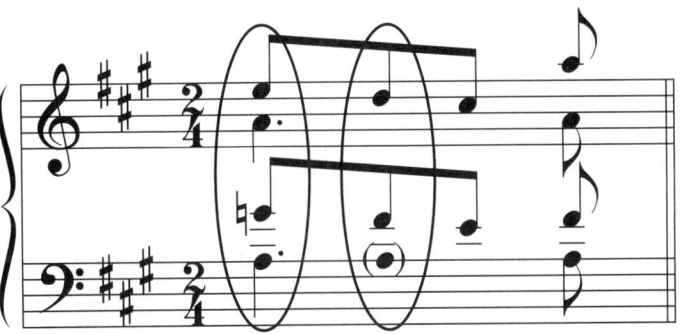

A Major: ____ / IV IV$^6_4$

4. The first half of the secondary dominant will be a dominant or dominant seventh chord. Label the first chord with V and the appropriate figured figured bass.

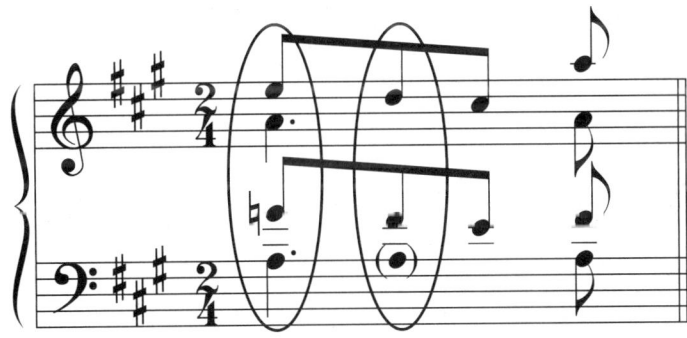

A Major: V^7 / IV IV$^6_4$

Excerpt from Schumann: *A Little Canon*

2. Name the Major or minor key for each of the following examples. Label each boxed chord with its Roman numeral and figured bass.

a. From *French Suite No. 1: Menuet,* by J.S. Bach. Key of: _____ minor

___ / ___ ___

b. From *Sonata, Hob. XVI:40,* by Haydn. Key of: _____ Major

___ / ___ ___

c. From *Sonata, K. 283,* by Mozart. Key of: _____ Major

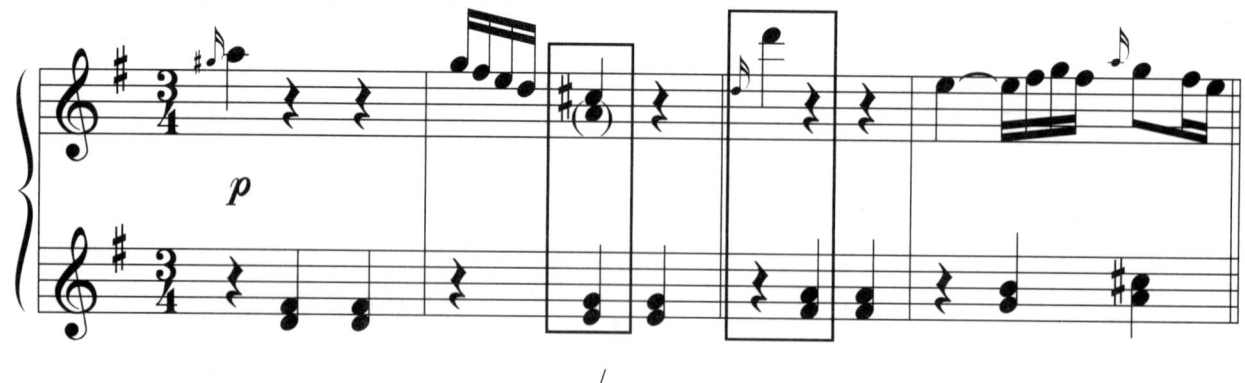

___ / ___ ___

d. From *Grillen* by Schumann. Key of: _____ Major

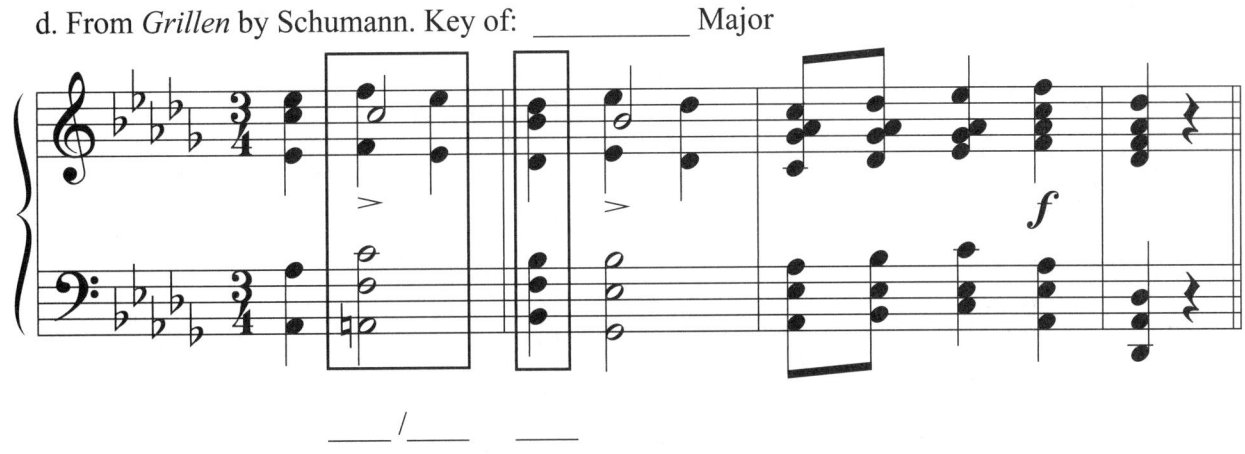

e. From *French Suite No. 3, Menuet II,* by J.S. Bach. Key of: _____ minor

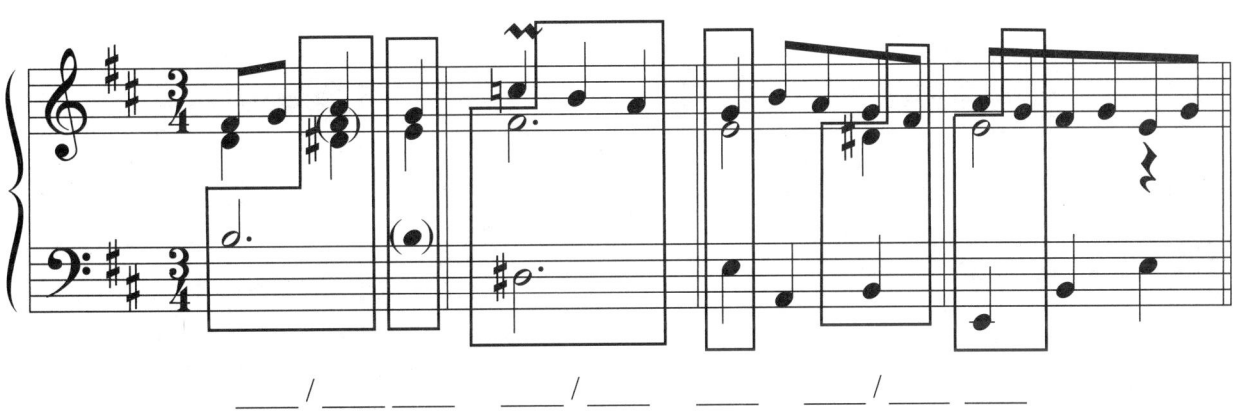

f. From *Sonata, K. 280,* by Mozart. Key of: _____ Major

g. From *Sonata, Hob. XVI:42,* by Haydn. Key of: _____ Major

____ of ____ ____

h. From *Sonata, Op. 2, No. 1,* by Beethoven. Key of _____ Major

____ of ____ ____

i. From *Sonata, Op. 2, No. 1,* by Beethoven. Key of: _____ Major

____ of ____ ____

LESSON 9
AUTHENTIC, HALF, PLAGAL, AND DECEPTIVE CADENCES; CHORD PROGRESSIONS

A <u>**CADENCE**</u> is a closing or ending for a musical phrase, made up of a combination of chords. There are many types of cadences. Four common cadences are:

AUTHENTIC, HALF, PLAGAL, and DECEPTIVE CADENCES

An <u>**AUTHENTIC CADENCE**</u> consists of a V or V^7 chord followed by a I chord:

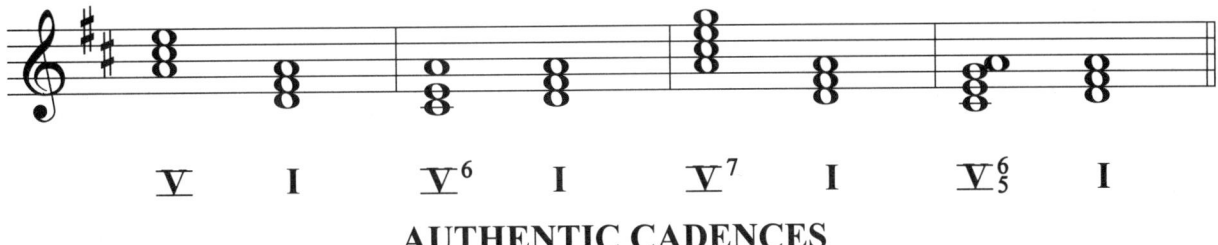

AUTHENTIC CADENCES

A <u>**PLAGAL CADENCE**</u> consists of a IV chord followed by a I chord:

PLAGAL CADENCES

A <u>**HALF CADENCE**</u> is a cadence which ends with a V or V^7 chord:

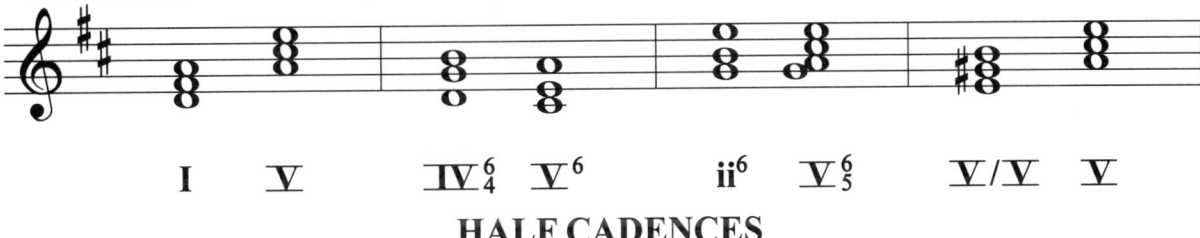

HALF CADENCES

A <u>**DECEPTIVE CADENCE**</u> consists of a V (or sometimes IV) chord followed by a vi chord:

DECEPTIVE CADENCES

1. Notate each of the following cadences. Determine whether to use the Major or minor key by the quality of the Roman numerals.

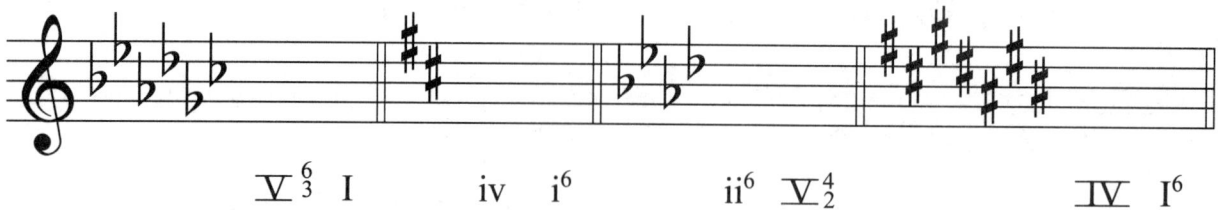

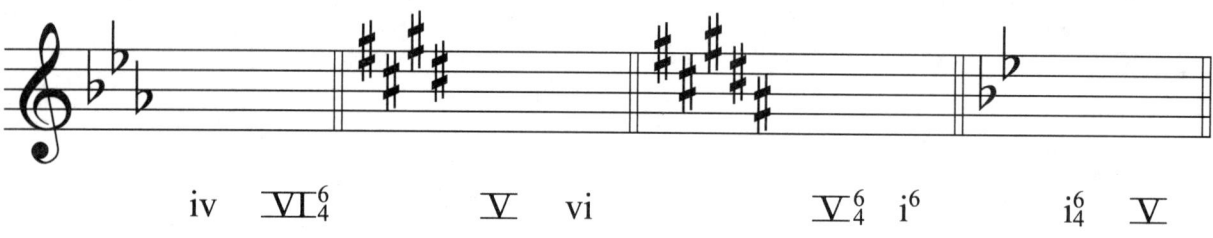

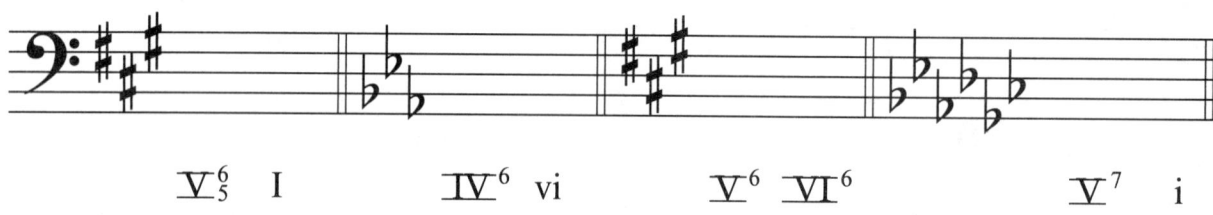

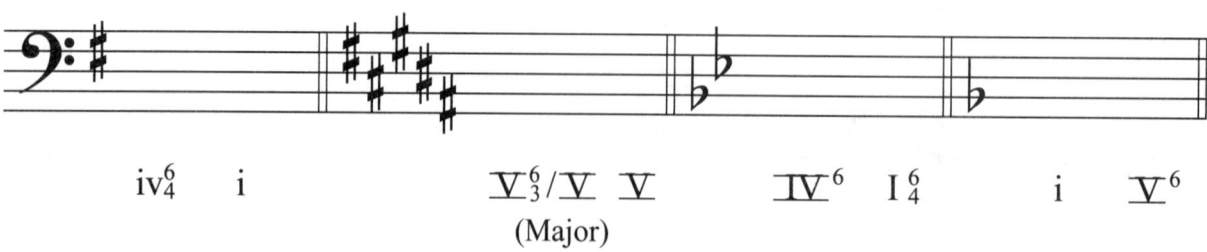

2. For each of the following examples, label the chords with Roman numerals and figured bass and write the name of the cadence (authentic, half, plagal, or deceptive).

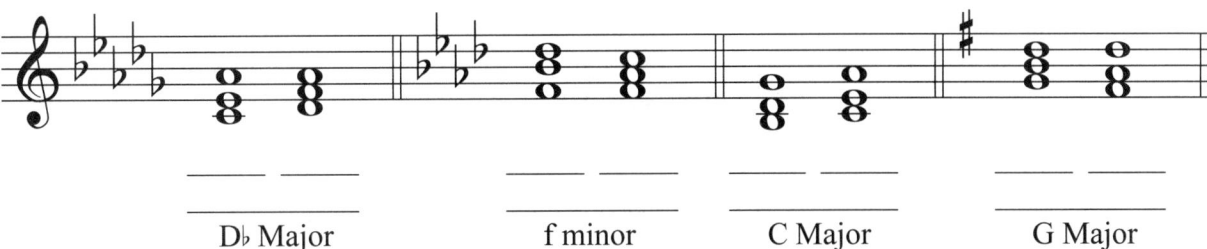

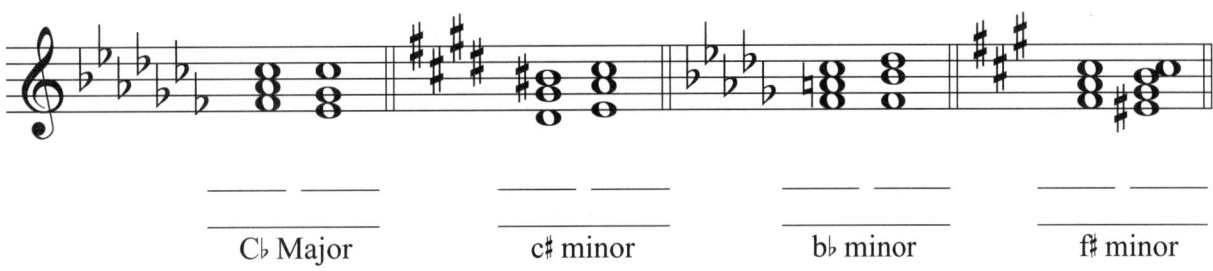

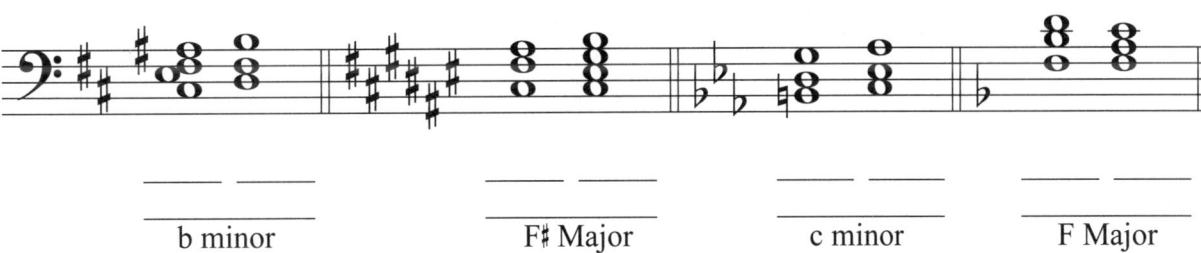

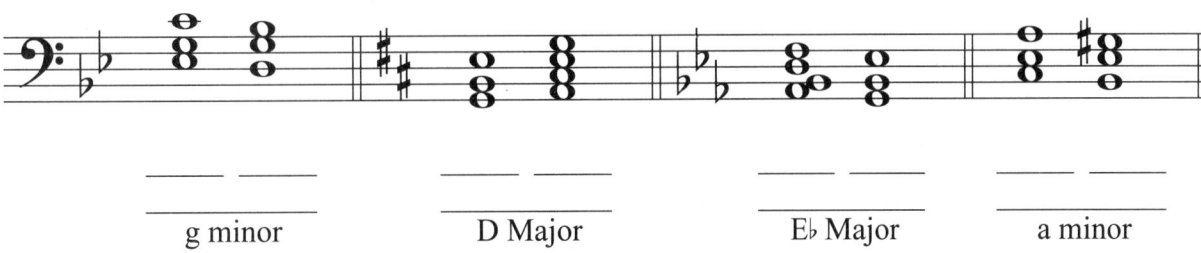

A **CHORD PROGRESSION** or **MIXED CADENCE** is created by combining certain chords within a key. A smooth progression is created by using **common tones** (notes that remain the same when the chord changes). The following chord progression **MODULATES** to a new key. (See more on modulation in Lesson 10.)

A **PIVOT CHORD** is used to transition to the new key. The pivot chord is common to both the original key and the key to which the music modulates.

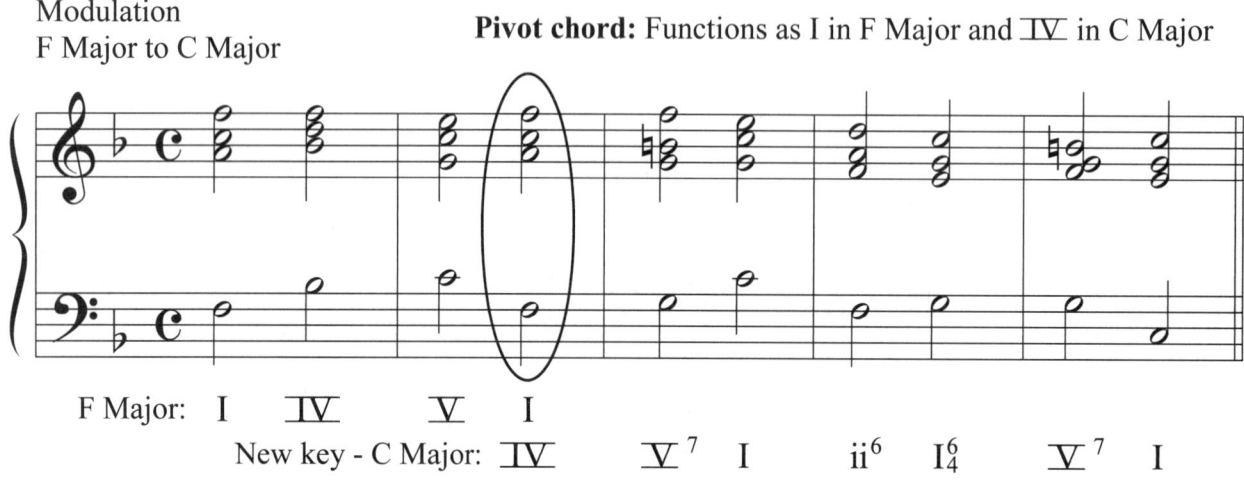

3. a. For each of the following chord progressions, label the chords with Roman Numerals and figured bass and circle the pivot chord.

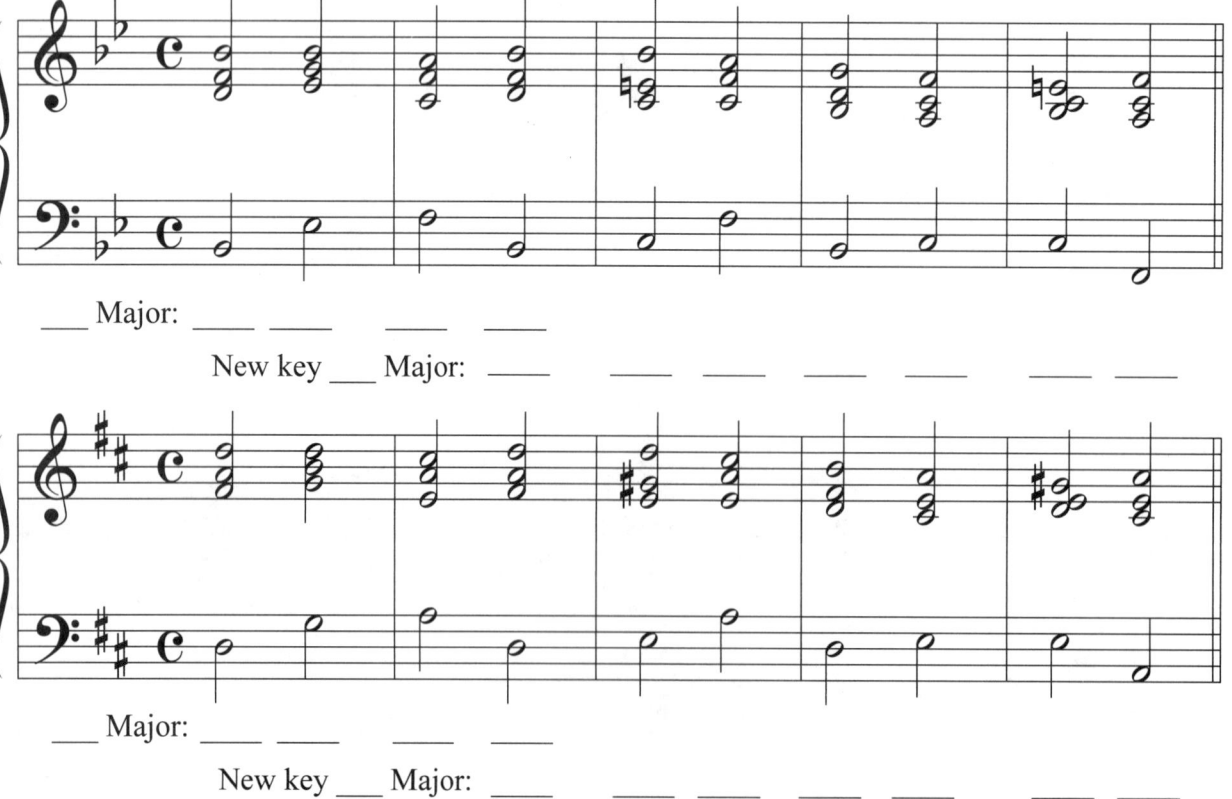

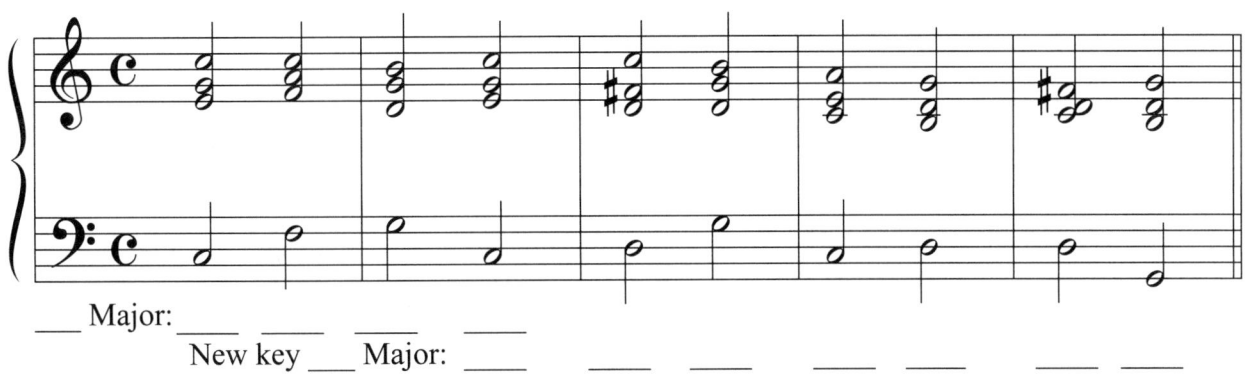

___ Major: ___ ___ ___ ___
New key ___ Major: ___

b. Notate each of the following chord progressions. Circle the pivot chord in each example.

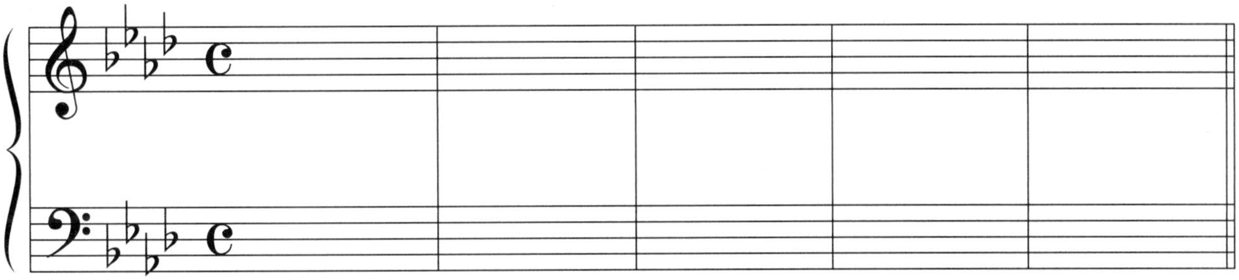

___ Major: I IV V I
New key ___ Major: IV V⁷ I ii⁶ I⁶₄ V⁷ I

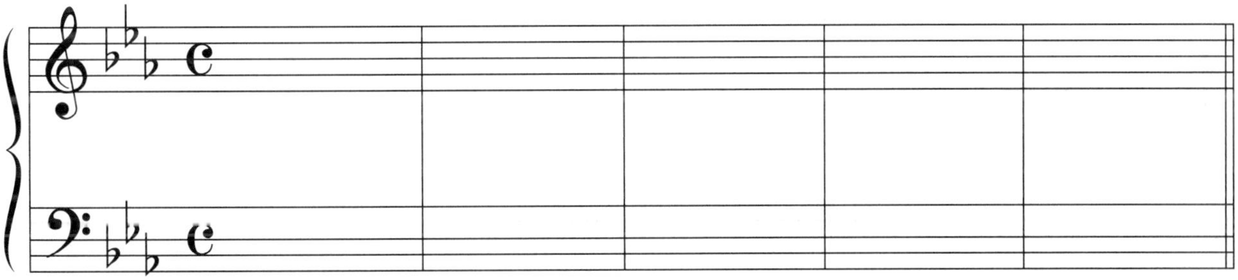

___ Major: I IV V I
New key ___ Major: IV V⁷ I ii⁶ I⁶₄ V⁷ I

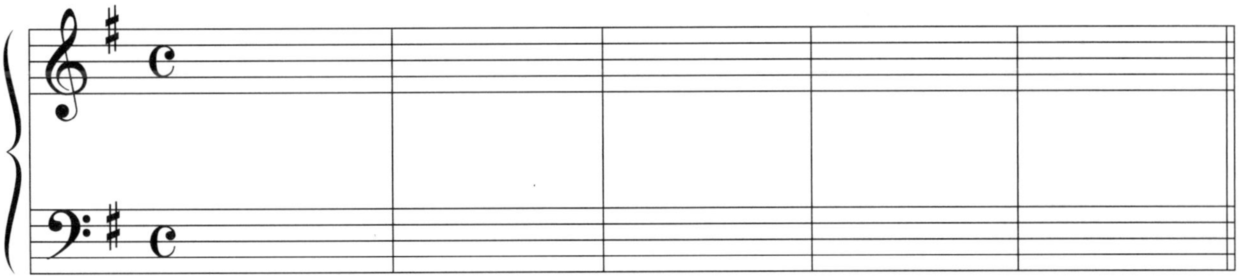

___ Major: I IV V I
New key ___ Major: IV V⁷ I ii⁶ I⁶₄ V⁷ I

To name cadences in a composition, label the last two chords of the phrase with Roman numerals and figured bass. Use these two chords to determine the cadence (authentic, half, plagal, or deceptive).

Example (From *Waltz, Op. posth. 69, No. 1,* by Chopin.): Key of A♭ Major, Authentic Cadence

4. For each of the following phrases, name the Major or minor key. Label the underlined chords with Roman numerals and figured bass and name the cadence that is formed by the chords.

a. From *Rhapsody, Op. 119, No. 4,* by Brahms.

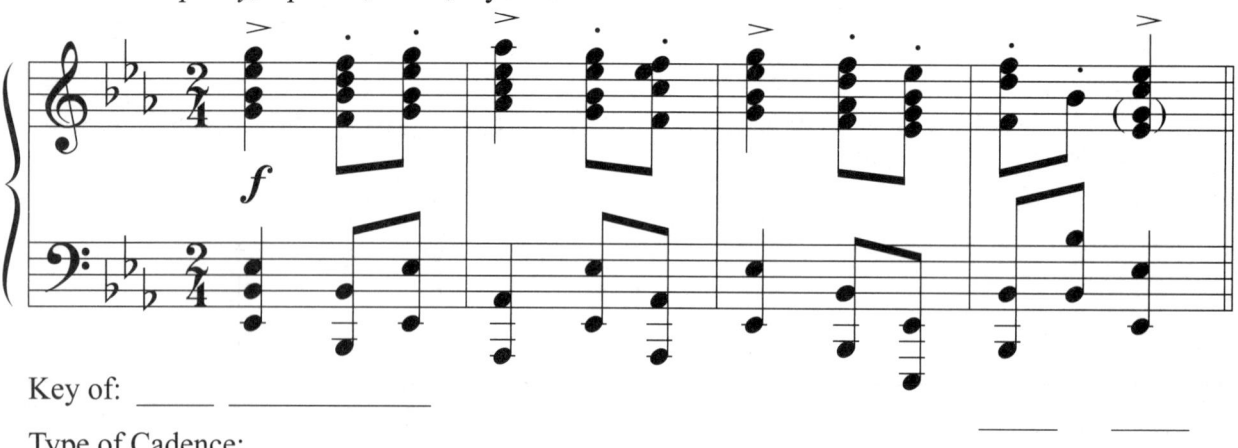

Key of: _____ _____

Type of Cadence: _____

b. From *Sonata, Op. 10, No. 1,* by Beethoven.

Key of: _____ _____

Type of Cadence: _____

c. From *Sonata, Op. 2, No. 1,* by Beethoven.

Key of: _____ _____   _____   _____

Type of Cadence: _____

d. From *Sonata, K. 281,* by Mozart.

Key of: _____ _____   _____   _____

Type of Cadence: _____

e. From *Sonata, K. 283,* by Mozart.

Key of: _____ _____   _____   _____

Type of Cadence: _____

f. From *Sonata, Hob. XVI:42* by Haydn.

Key of: _____ _____

Type of Cadence: _____

g. From *Sonata No. 32* by Scarlatti.

Key of: _____ _____

Type of Cadence: _____

h. From *Sonata, . 284,* by Mozart.

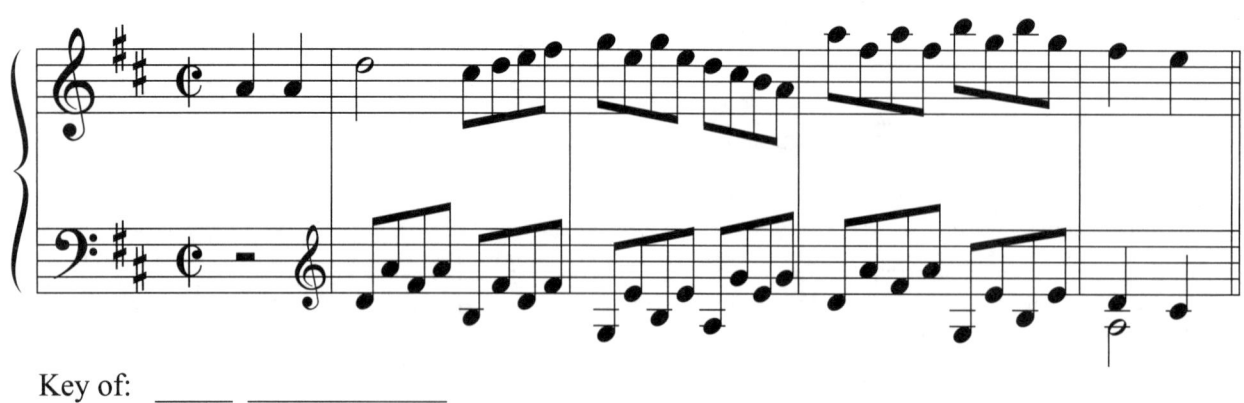

Key of: _____ _____

Type of Cadence: _____

LESSON 10
MODULATION

MODULATION occurs when a musical composition changes from the original key to another key, and remains in the new key for a reasonable amount of time.

Music may modulate to any key, but frequently the dominant (V) or the relative Major or minor is used.

In the example below from *Sonatina, Op. 36, No. 3* by Clementi, the music begins in the key of D Major and modulates to the key of A Major.

Two important 20th Century theorists, Schoenberg and Schenker, taught that music does not modulate. Further study of Schenkerian Analysis is recommended.

1. For each of the following excerpts, name the original key and the key to which the music modulates.

a. From *Sonata, Hob. XVI:41,* by Haydn.

   Original key: _____ Modulates to: _____

b. From *Sonata, K. 279,* by Mozart.

Original key: _____ Modulates to: _____

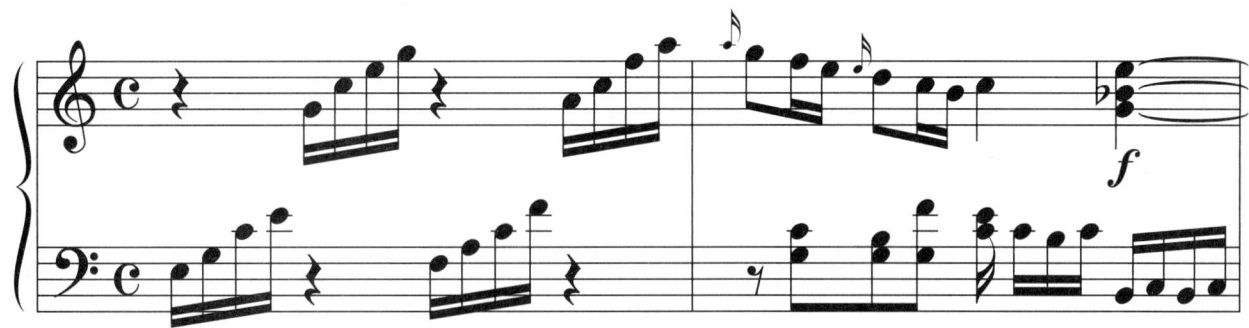

(continued on p. 72)

c. From *Intermezzo, Op. 118, No. 2,* by Brahms.

Original key: _____ Modulates to: _____

d. From *Sonata (1766)* by Haydn.

Original key: _____ Modulates to: _____

REVIEW
TERMS USED IN LESSONS 1-10

Aeolian mode: scale with the same pattern of whole and half steps that occurs when beginning and ending on the sixth note of the major scale; half steps occur between notes 2-3 and 5-6; aeolian mode is the same as natural minor

authentic cadence: a V-I cadence; in harmomic minor, V-i

cadence: a closing or ending for a phrase of music, made up of two or more chords

chromatic half step: 1. a half step which does not occur naturally within the key of the music; 2. a half step written using two notes with the same letter name

chromatic scale: a scale made up entirely of half steps

deceptive cadence: a V-vi cadence; in harmonic minor, V-VI

diatonic half step: 1. a half step which occurs naturally within the key of the music; 2. a half step written using two notes with different letter names

diminished seventh chord: a four note chord made up of a diminished triad and a diminished 7th above the root

dominant seventh: a four note chord made up of a Major triad, and a minor 7th above the root. Root position is V^7, first inversion is V^6_5, second inversion is V^4_3, and third inversion is V^4_2 or V^2

Dorian mode: scale with the same pattern of whole and half steps that occurs when beginning and ending on the second note of the major scale; half steps occur between notes 2-3 and 6-7

figured bass: symbols that indicate the inversion of a chord, such as $^6_4$

first inversion: a triad written with the third as the lowest note; figured bass for a triad in first inversion is $^6_3$ or ^{6}; figured bass for a seventh chord in first inversion is $^6_5$

half cadence: a cadence which ends with the V chord

half diminished seventh chord: a four note chord made up of a diminished triad and the interval of a minor seventh

interval: the distance between two notes named with qualities and numbers; intervals may be Major, Perfect, minor, diminished, or Augmented

inversion: a triad written in a position in which the note that names the triad is not the lowest

Ionian mode: scale with the same pattern of whole and half steps that occurs when beginning and ending on the first note of the major scale; half steps occur between notes 3-4 and 7-8; Ionian mode is the same as the major scale

key signature: sharps or flats at the beginning of the music that indicate tonality and which notes receive sharps or flats

Locrian mode: scale with the same pattern of whole and half steps that occurs when beginning and ending on the seventh note of the major scale; half steps occur between notes 1-2 and 4-5

Lydian mode: scale with the same pattern of whole and half steps that occurs when beginning and ending on the fourth note of the major scale; half steps occur between notes 4-5 and 7-8

major seventh chord: a four note chord made up of a Major triad and the interval of a Major seventh

minor seventh chord: a four note chord made up of a minor triad and the interval of a minor seventh

Mixolydian mode: scale with the same pattern of whole and half steps that occurs when beginning and ending on the fifth note of the major scale; half steps occur between notes 3-4 and 6-7

modes: tonalities including but not limited to Ionian, Dorian, Phrygian, Lydian, Mixolydian, Aeolian, and Locrian

modulation: a key change within a composition

Phrygian mode: scale with the same pattern of whole and half steps that occurs when beginning and ending on the third note of the major scale; half steps occur between notes 1-2 and 5-6

pivot chord: used before a modulation, a chord that is common to both the original and the key to which the music modulates

plagal cadence: a IV-I cadence; in harmonic minor, iv-i

primary triads: the I, IV, and V chords; in minor, i, iv, and V

root position: a triad written in a position so that the note which names it is the lowest; figured bass for a triad in root position is $^5_3$; figured bass for a seventh chord in root position is ^{7}

scale: an organized sequence of notes upon which a composition is based

scale degree names: Tonic (I), Supertonic (ii), Mediant (iii), Subdominant (IV), Dominant (V), Submediant (vi), Leading Tone (vii°)

second inversion: a triad written with the fifth as the lowest note; figured bass for a triad in second inversion is $^6_4$; figured bass for a seventh chord in second inversion is $^4_3$

secondary dominant: the V or dominant of a key other than Tonic (I).

secondary triads: the ii, iii, vi, and vii° chords; in harmonic minor, ii°, III⁺/III, VI, and vii°

third inversion: a seventh chord written with the seventh as the lowest note; figured bass for third inversion is ^{2} or $^4_2$

triad: a three note chord based on the interval of a third with the quality Major, minor, Augmented, or diminished

whole tone scale: a scale made up entirely of whole steps

REVIEW
LESSONS 1-10

1. Write the name of the Major key for each of the following key signatures.

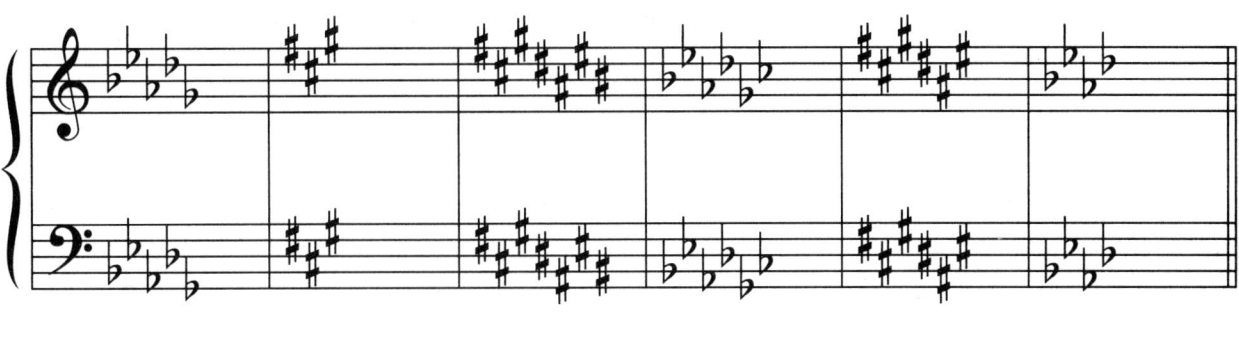

_____ _____ _____ _____ _____ _____

2. Write the name of the minor key for each of the following key signatures.

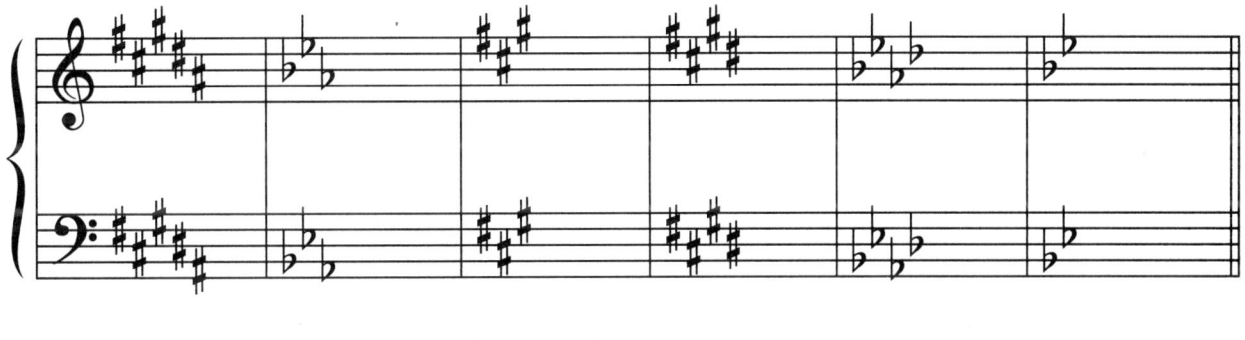

_____ _____ _____ _____ _____ _____

3. Notate the key signature for each of the following keys in both clefs.

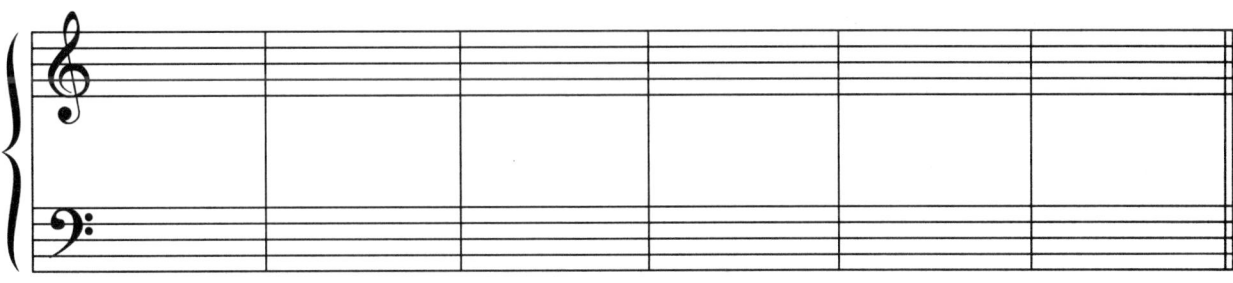

C♭ Major   C♯ Major   b♭ minor   d minor   E Major   b minor

4. Complete the Circle of Fifths. Write the name for each Major and minor key including enharmonic keys, and notate the key signatures.

5. Notate each of the following scales.

e melodic minor (ascending and descending)

Chromatic beginning on D (ascending and descending)

g natural minor

c# harmonic minor

Whole tone beginning on G

A♭ Major

Aeolian mode on E

Locrian mode on F#

6. Name each of the following intervals with its quality and number.

___   ___   ___   ___   ___   ___   ___   ___

7. Complete each of the following intervals.

m3 up   A5 down   P8 up   m2 down   d4 up   M6 up   m7 up   d4 down

8. Notate half-steps above each of the following notes using two different letter names (diatonic half-steps).

9. Notate half-steps above each of the following notes using the same letter name (chromatic half- steps).

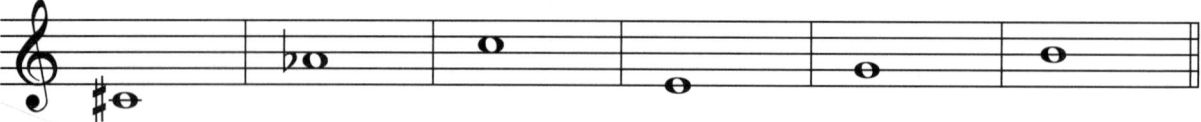

10. Label each of the following triads with its root, quality, and figured bass.

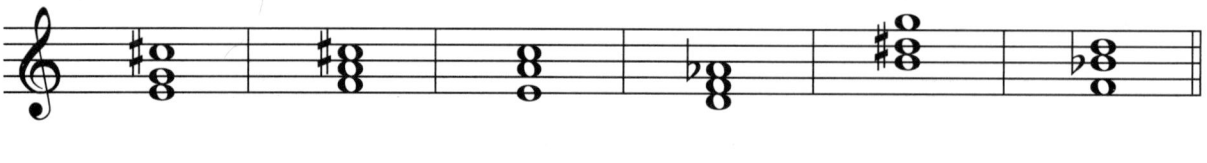

___   ___   ___   ___   ___   ___

11. Notate each of the following triads.

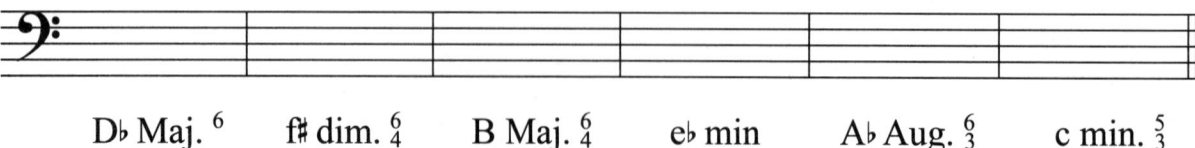

D♭ Maj. ^{6} f♯ dim. $^6_4$ B Maj. $^6_4$ e♭ min   A♭ Aug. $^6_3$ c min. $^5_3$

12. Notate the primary triads for each of the following keys and label the triads with Roman numerals.

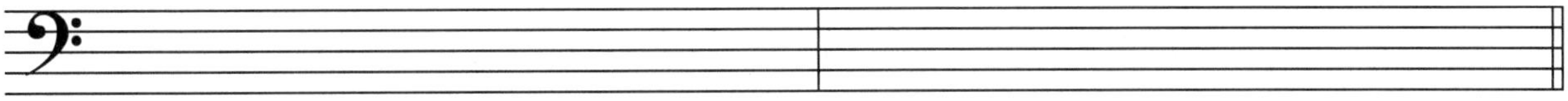

a minor					G Major

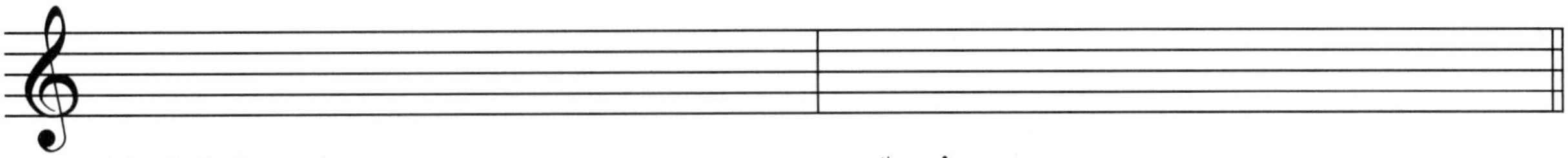

A♭ Major					c♯ minor

13. Notate the secondary triads for each of the following keys and label the triads with Roman numerals.

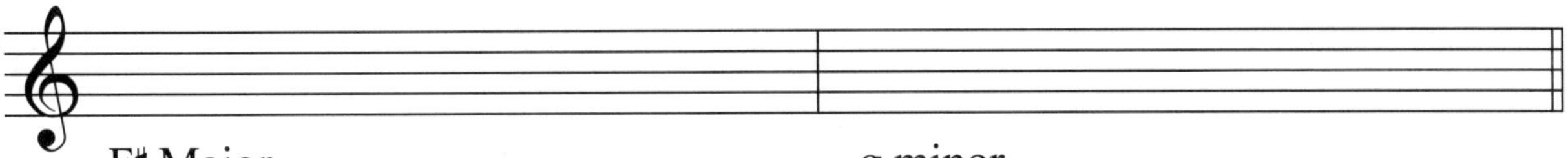

F♯ Major					g minor

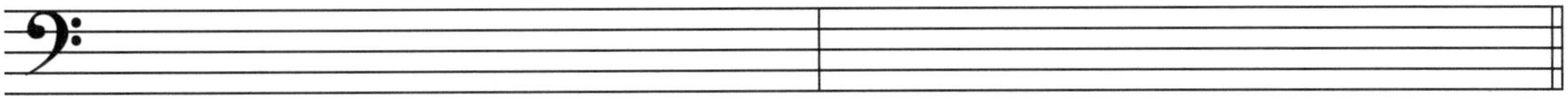

b minor					D Major

14. Notate the triads of the whole tone scale beginning on each of the following notes.

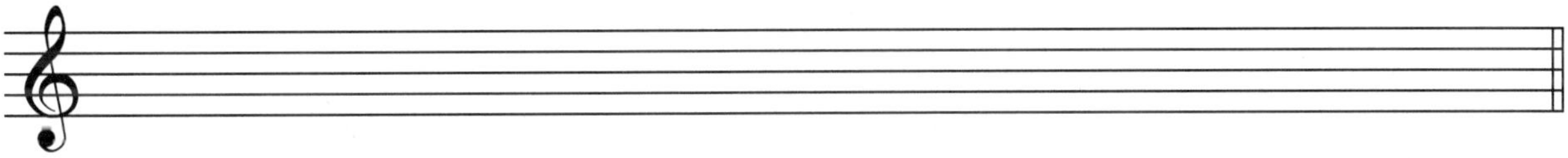

Beginning on C♯

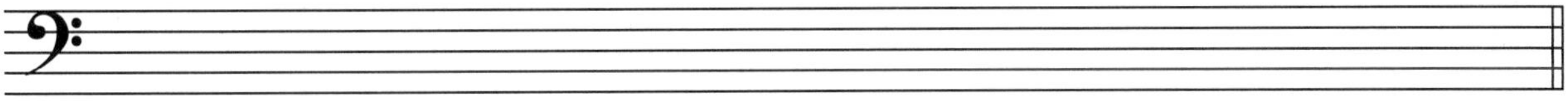

Beginning on A♭

15. Write the scale degree name for each of the following Roman numerals.

a. I or i _____		e. V _____
b. ii or ii° _____		f. V^7 _____
c. iii or III$^+$/III _____	g. vi or VI _____
d. IV or iv _____		h. vii° _____

16. Name each of the following seventh chords with its root, quality, and figured bass.

_____   _____   _____   _____   _____   _____

17. Notate each of the following seventh chords.

c♯ min. $\frac{4}{3}$ f min. $\frac{6}{5}$ A Maj. $\frac{4}{2}$ E♭ Dom. ^{2} b min. ^{7} F♯ Dom. $\frac{4}{3}$

18. Using the Major key for each example, label each of the following secondary dominants and its resolution with Roman numerals and figured bass.

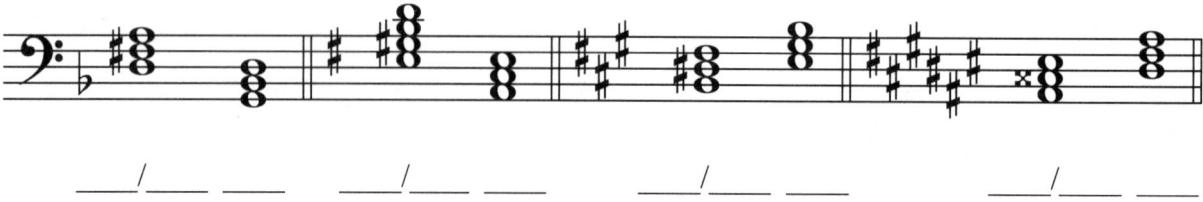

___/___ ___   ___/___ ___   ___/___ ___   ___/___ ___

19 Notate each of the following secondary dominants and its resolution.

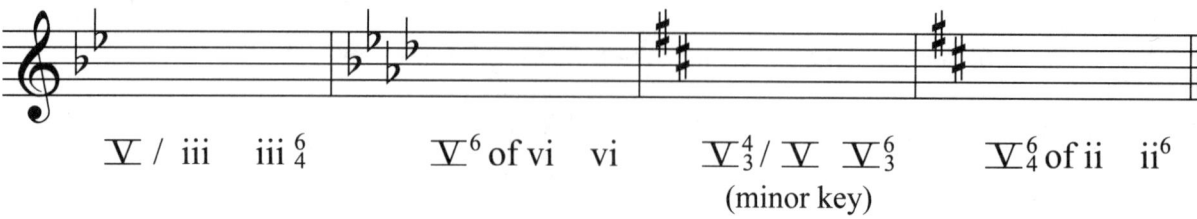

V / iii   iii $\frac{6}{4}$ V^6 of vi   vi   V$\frac{4}{3}$/ V   V$\frac{6}{3}$ V$\frac{6}{4}$ of ii   ii^6
                              (minor key)

20. Label the following chords with Roman numerals and figured bass and name the cadence formed by each pair of chords.

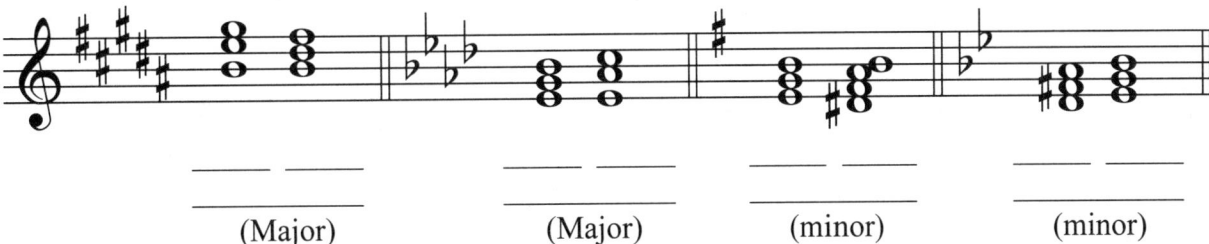

(Major) (Major) (minor) (minor)

21. Notate each of the following cadences.

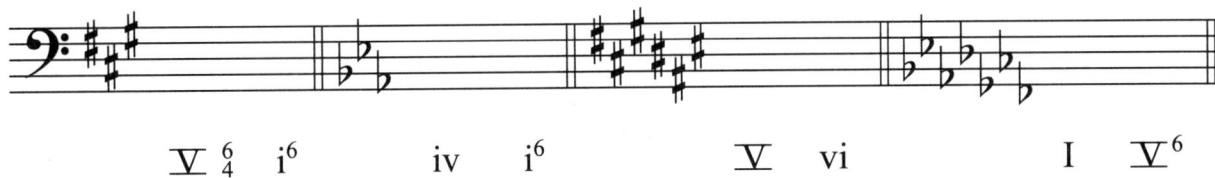

V_4^6 i^6 iv i^6 V vi   I V^6

22. Notate each of the following chord progressions.

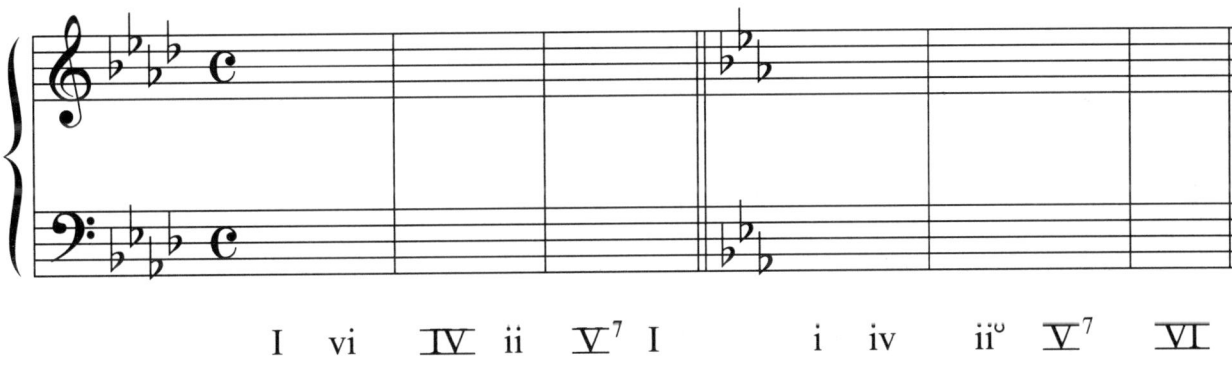

I vi IV ii V^7 I   i iv ii° V^7 VI

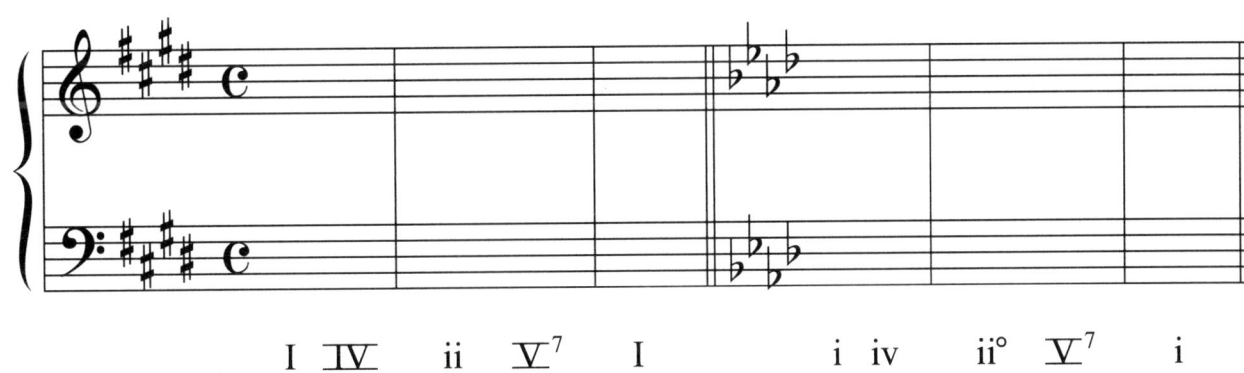

I IV ii V^7 I   i iv ii° V^7 i

23. The following example is from *Sinfonia No. 2* by J.S. Bach. Answer the questions about the music.

a. What is the key or tonality? _____ _____

b. Which form of minor is used in measures 1-2? _____

c. Name each circled interval with its quality and number.

   1. _____ 2. _____ 3. _____ 4. _____ 5. _____

d. Name each boxed chord with its root, quality, Roman numeral, and figured bass. Do not include the notes that are in parantheses when determining the names of the chords.

	ROOT	QUALITY	ROMAN NUMERAL AND FIGURED BASS
Chord a.	_____	_____	_____
Chord b.	_____	_____	_____
Chord c.	_____	_____	_____

24. The following example is from *Nocturne, Op. 32, No. 1*, by Chopin. Answer the questions about the music.

a. What is the key or tonality? _____ _____

b. Name each circled interval with its quality and number.

1. _____ 2. _____ 3. _____ 4. _____ 5. _____ 6. _____ 7. _____

c. Name each boxed chord with its root, quality, Roman numeral, and figured bass. Do not include the notes that are in parantheses when determining the names of the chords.

	ROOT	**QUALITY**	**ROMAN NUMERAL AND FIGURED BASS**
Chord a.	_____	_____	_____
Chord b.	_____	_____	_____
Chord c.	_____	_____	_____
Chord d.	_____	_____	_____
Chord e.	_____	_____	_____

d. What is the term for chord **a**? _____

e. What type of cadence is used in measures 3-4? _____

25. The following example is from *Sonata, K. 284,* by Mozart. Answer the questions about the music.

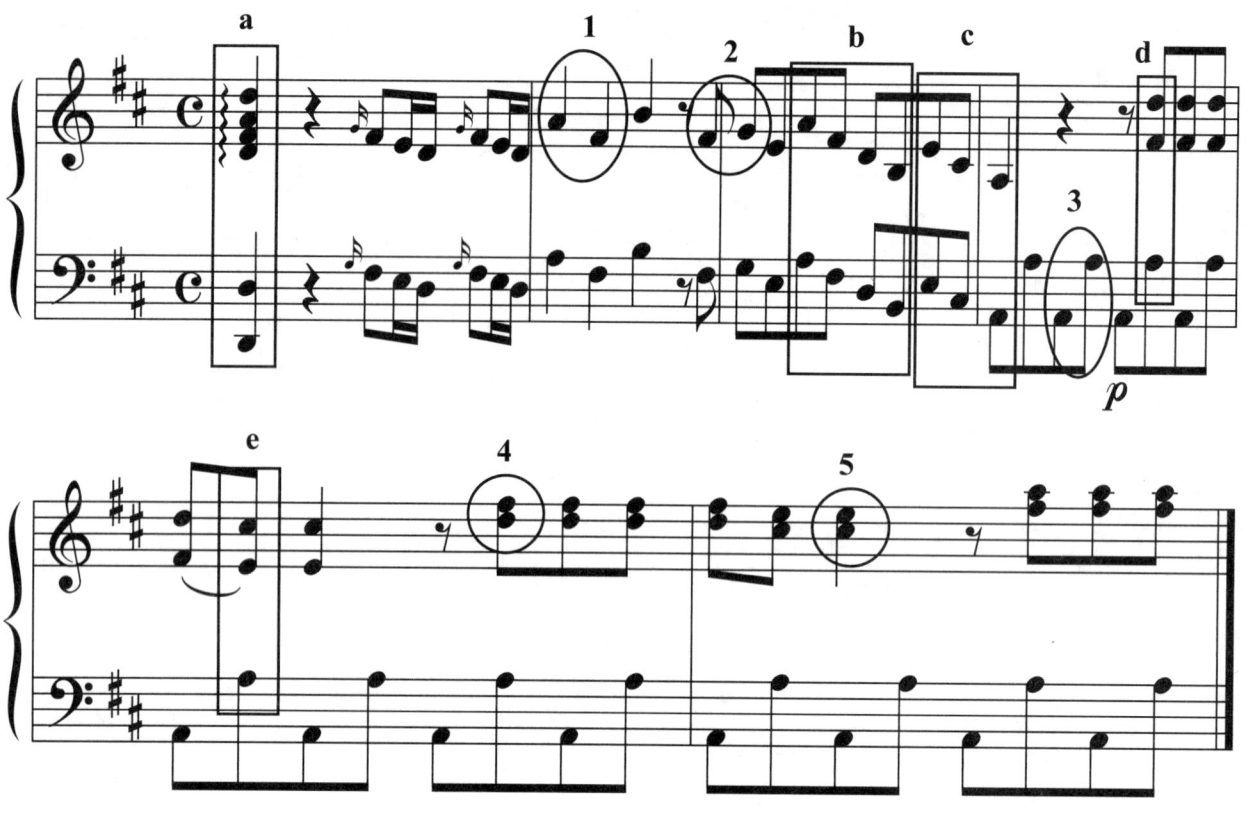

a. What is the key or tonality? _____ _____

b. Name each circled interval with its quality and number.

1. _____ 2. _____ 3. _____ 4. _____ 5. _____

c. Name each boxed chord with its root, quality, Roman numeral, and figured bass.

	ROOT	QUALITY	ROMAN NUMERAL AND FIGURED BASS
Chord a.	_____	_____	_____
Chord b.	_____	_____	XXXXXX
Chord c.	_____	_____	_____
Chord d.	_____	_____	_____
Chord e.	_____	_____	_____

LESSON 11
TIME SIGNATURES

The **TIME SIGNATURE** for a composition is found at the beginning of the music, to the right of the key signature. The time signature is often made up of two numbers:

The symbol 𝐂 or ₵ may be used instead of numbers.

𝐂 stands for $\frac{4}{4}$, or **Common Time.**

₵ stands for $\frac{2}{2}$, or **Alla Breve.**

The top number of the time signature indicates the number of beats in each measure.

The bottom number indicates which type of note receives one beat.

2 = 2 beats per measure
4 = Quarter note (♩) receives one beat

3 = 3 beats per measure
8 = Eighth note (♪) receives one beat

METER is determined by the time signature, and refers to the division of beats into equal groups, such as three beats per measure in $\frac{3}{4}$ time.

When the bottom number of a time signature is a "4," a quarter note (♩) receives one beat. The following chart shows how many beats to give these notes or rests (other forms of counting are possible):

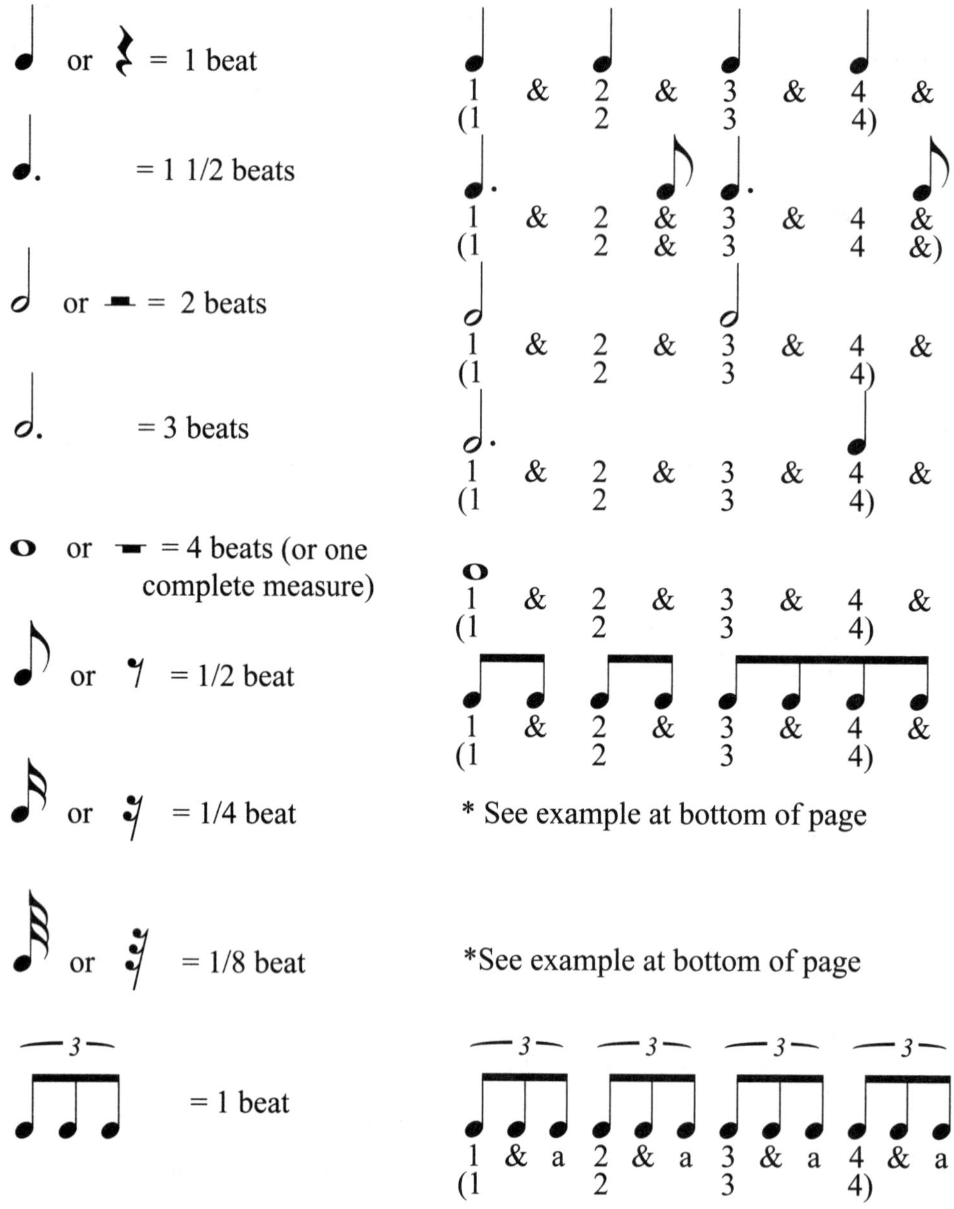

♩ or 𝄽 = 1 beat

♩. = 1 1/2 beats

𝅗𝅥 or 𝄼 = 2 beats

𝅗𝅥. = 3 beats

𝅝 or 𝄻 = 4 beats (or one complete measure)

♪ or 𝄾 = 1/2 beat

𝅘𝅥𝅯 or 𝄿 = 1/4 beat

𝅘𝅥𝅰 or 𝅀 = 1/8 beat

𝅘𝅥𝅯𝅘𝅥𝅯𝅘𝅥𝅯 (triplet) = 1 beat

*See example at bottom of page

*See example at bottom of page

*Counting for some of the more common eighth, sixteenth, and thirty-second note patterns is shown here:

Double dot: If a note has two dots, the second dot is worth half the value of the first dot.

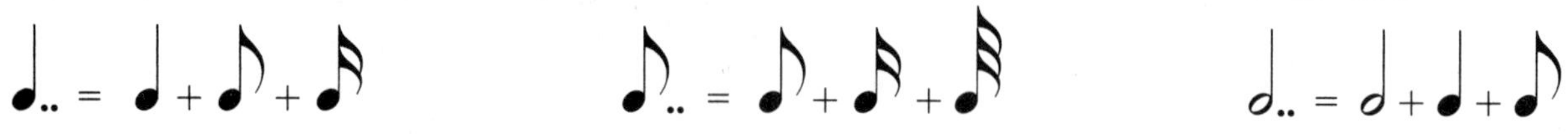

An **UPBEAT** occurs when the first measure is incomplete. The last beat or beats are "borrowed" from the final measure and placed at the beginning. The beats used for the upbeat measure will be the last numbers of the time signature. The final measure will have fewer beats than normal. The first full measure begins with count number 1.

Example:

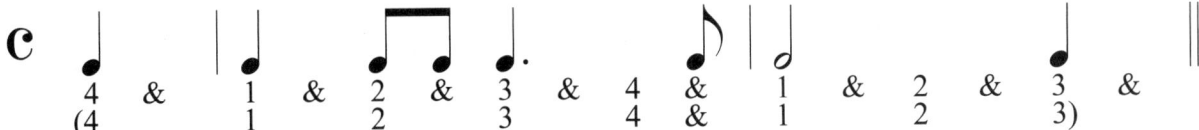

When the bottom number of a time signature is a "2," a half note (𝅗𝅥) receives one beat. The following chart shows how many beats to give these notes or rests (other forms of counting are possible):

𝅗𝅥 or 𝄼	= 1 beat	𝅗𝅥 𝅗𝅥 → 1 & 2 & (1 2)
𝅗𝅥.	= 1 1/2 beats	𝅗𝅥. 𝅘𝅥 → 1 & 2 & (1 2 &)
𝅝 or 𝄻	= 2 beats	𝅝 → 1 & 2 & (1 2)
𝅘𝅥 or 𝄽	= 1/2 beat	𝅘𝅥 𝅘𝅥 𝅘𝅥 𝅘𝅥 → 1 & 2 & (1 2)
𝅘𝅥𝅮 or 𝄾	= 1/4 beat	𝅘𝅥𝅮𝅘𝅥𝅮𝅘𝅥𝅮𝅘𝅥𝅮 𝅘𝅥 𝅘𝅥𝅮𝅘𝅥𝅮 → 1 e & a 2 e & a (1 2)
𝅘𝅥𝅯 or 𝄿	= 1/8 beat	𝅘𝅥𝅯𝅘𝅥𝅯𝅘𝅥𝅯𝅘𝅥𝅯𝅘𝅥𝅯𝅘𝅥𝅯 𝅘𝅥𝅮 𝅘𝅥 → 1 e & a 2 & (1 2)
𝅘𝅥𝅰 or 𝅀	= 1/16 beat	𝅘𝅥𝅰𝅘𝅥𝅰𝅘𝅥𝅰𝅘𝅥𝅰𝅘𝅥𝅰𝅘𝅥𝅰𝅘𝅥𝅯𝅘𝅥𝅮 → 1 e & a

An 8 as the bottom number of a time signature indicates that an eighth note (♪) receives one beat. However, time signatures with a bottom number of 8 have basic beats of a dotted quarter note (♩.) with three sub-beats within each basic beat (other forms of counting are possible):

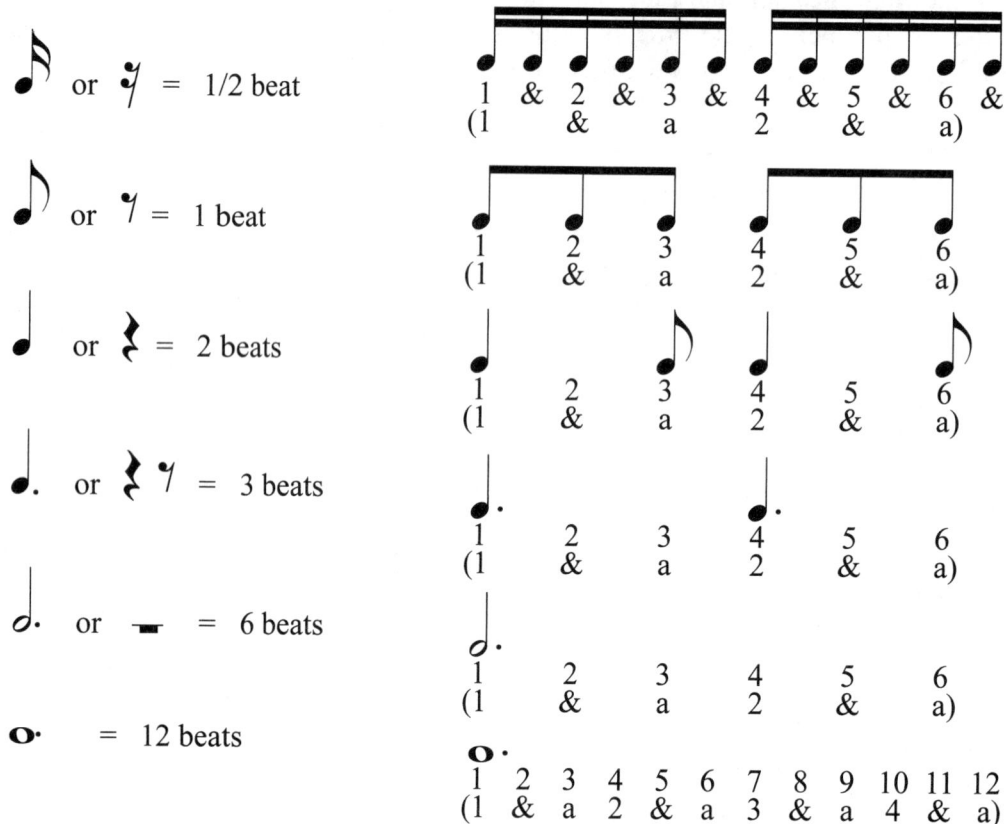

1. Fill in the blanks. The first one is given.

2 = _2 beats per measure_
4 = _Quarter note receives one beat_

3 = _____
4 = _____

3 = _____
8 = _____

¢ = _____

C = _____

2 = _____
2 = _____

7 = _____
4 = _____

6 = _____
8 = _____

When a time signature has a 2 on top ($\frac{2}{2}$, $\frac{2}{4}$, etc.), the first beat of the measure is strongest. There are two pulses per measure.

When a time signature has a 3 on top ($\frac{3}{8}$, $\frac{3}{4}$, etc.), the first beat of the measure is strongest. There are three pulses per measure.

When a time signature has a 4 on top ($\frac{4}{2}$, $\frac{4}{4}$, etc.), the first beat of the measure is strongest, and the third beat is slightly emphasized. There are four pulses per measure.

When a time signature has a 6 on top ($\frac{6}{8}$, $\frac{6}{4}$, etc.), the first beat of the measure is strongest, and the fourth beat is slightly emphasized. There are **two large pulses** per measure, each containing three smaller beats.

When a time signature has a 9 on top ($\frac{9}{8}$, $\frac{9}{4}$, etc.), the first beat of each measure is strongest, and the fourth and seventh beats are slightly emphasized. There are **three large pulses** per measure, each containing three smaller beats.

> *The accents in these rhythm patterns are only intended to demonstrate where strong and weak beats occur within the given meter. They are not meant to imply that every strong beat receives an accent.

When a time signature has a 12 on top ($\frac{12}{8}$, $\frac{12}{4}$, etc.), the first beat of each measure is strongest, and the fourth, seventh, and tenth beats are slightly emphasized. There are **four large pulses** per measure, each containing three smaller beats.

When a time signature has a 5 or 7 on top, the accented beats are irregular. Music in $\frac{5}{4}$, $\frac{5}{8}$, etc., will be divided into groups of 2 + 3 or 3 + 2. Music which is in $\frac{7}{4}$, $\frac{7}{8}$, etc., will be divided into groups of 4 + 3 or 3 + 4.

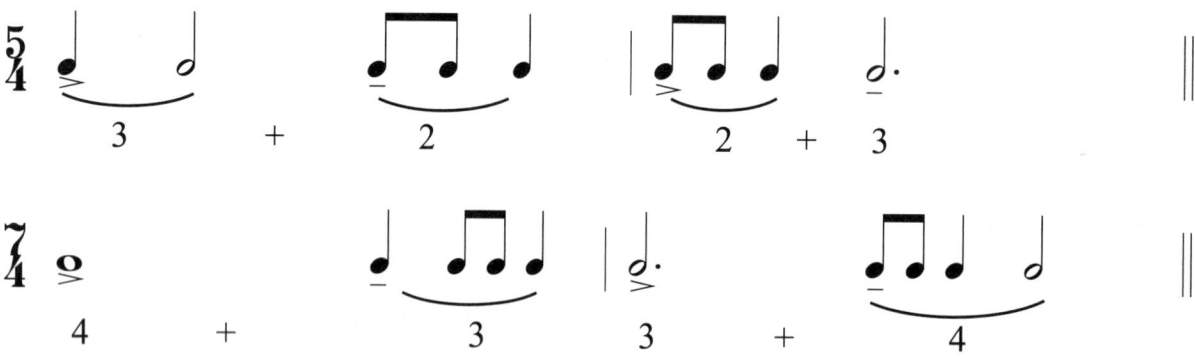

SYNCOPATION is a contradiction of the meter or pulse, often by changing strong and weak beats within the measure.

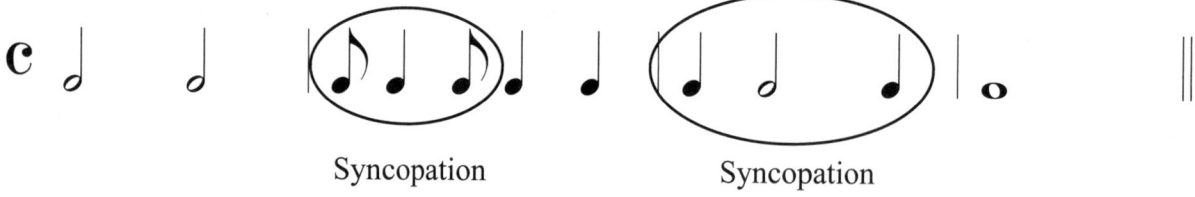

HEMIOLA occurs when the meter changes from two pulses per measure to three pulses by changing, for example, from $\frac{6}{8}$ to $\frac{3}{4}$ (Example A), or by the use of ties (Example B).

Example A   Example B

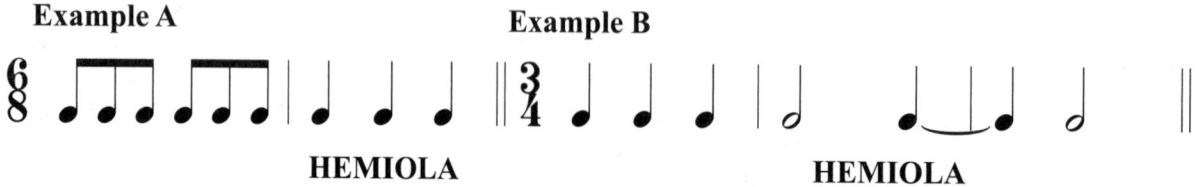

HEMIOLA   **HEMIOLA**

2. For each of the following phrases write the number of pulses in each measure, write counts between the treble clef and bass clef, and place accents on the strong beats.

a. From *Invention No. 14* by J.S. Bach. _____ pulses per measure

b. From *Rhapsody, Op. 119, No. 4,* by Brahms. _____ pulses per measure

c. From *Sinfonia No. 9* by J.S. Bach. _____ pulses per measure

d. From *Sonata No. 31* by Scarlatti. _____ pulses per measure

e. From *Sonata, Op. 10, No. 1,* by Beethoven. _____ pulses per measure

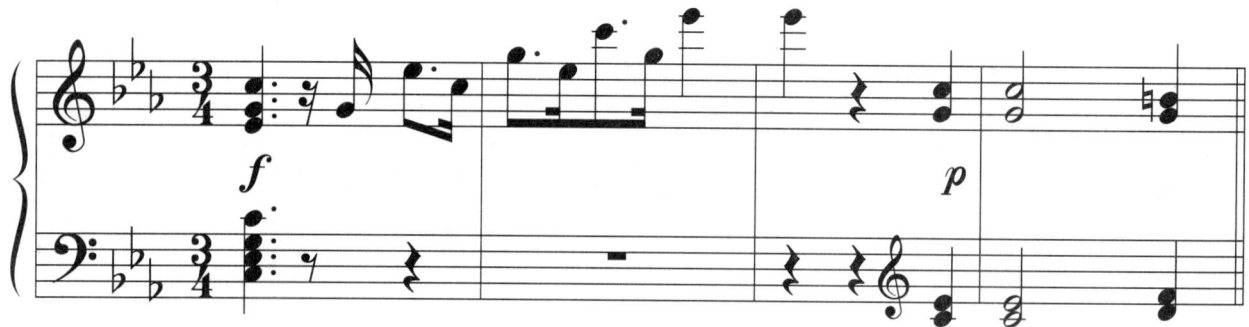

f. From *Sonata, Hob. XVI:49,* by Haydn. _____ pulses per measure

g. From *Sonata, XVI:34,* by Haydn. _____ pulses per measure

h. From *Sonata, XVI:40,* by Haydn _____ pulses per measure

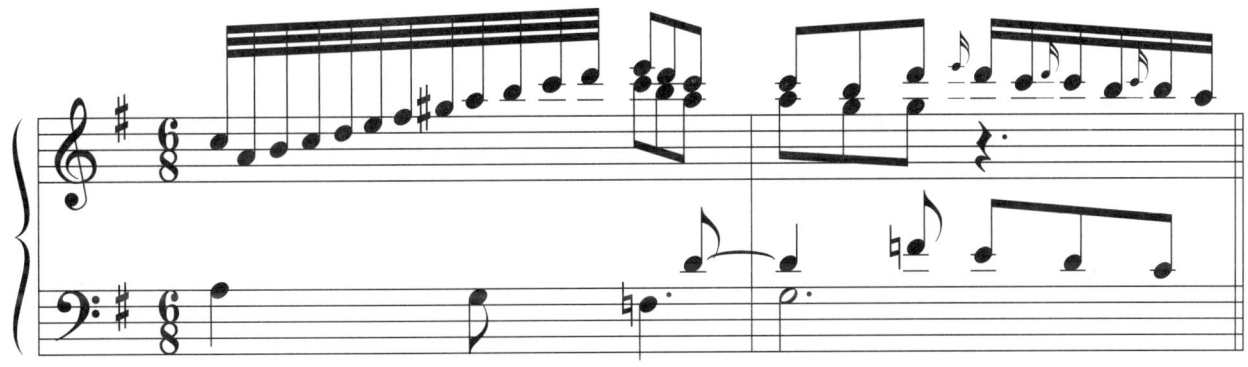

i. From *Sonata, XVI:42* by Haydn. _____ pulses per measure

j. From *Sonata, K. 281,* by Mozart. _____ pulses per measure

k. From *Sonata, K. 283,* by Mozart. _____ pulses per measure

l. From *Sonata, XVI:42* by Haydn. _____ pulses per measure

3. Define each of the following terms.

a. Meter _____

b. Syncopation _____

c. Hemiola _____

LESSON 12
HOMOPHONIC AND POLYPHONIC TEXTURES

TEXTURE is the manner in which the various voices or parts of music are put together. Music consists of vertical elements (harmony), and horizontal elements (melody). How these two components are woven together create the texture.

CONTRAPUNTAL or **POLYPHONIC TEXTURE** occurs when there are two or more voices that are of equal importance. The melodies are passed between the voices. This example, from *Sinfonia No. 3* by J.S. Bach, shows the use of polyphonic texture (or **Counterpoint**).

HOMOPHONIC TEXTURE occurs when there is one voice which dominates the music, while the other voice or voices serve as an accompaniment. Homophonic texture may have a **separate melody and accompaniment,** or may be **chordal**. This example, from *Sonata, Op. 10, No. 1,* by Beethoven, shows the use of homophonic texture.

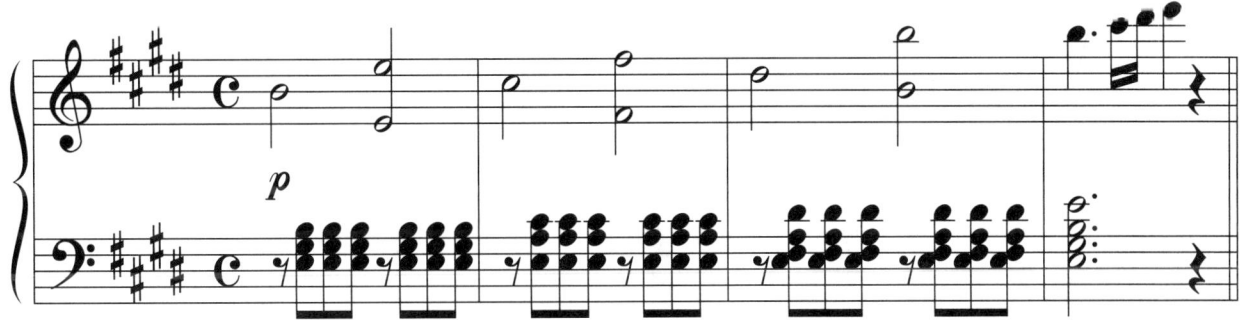

*Some theory scholars divide texture into three categories: Homophonic, polyphonic, and chordal. The term Homorhythmic is sometimes used to describe chordal texture in which each beat has a chord, such as in a four part hymn.

1. Name the texture for each of the following phrases.

a. From *Nocturne, Op. posth. 72, No. 1,* by Chopin. _____ texture

b. From *French Suite No. 1: Menuet,* by J.S. Bach. _____ texture

c. From *Rhapsody, Op. 119, No. 4,* by Brahms. _____ texture

d. From *Sonata, K. 284,* by Mozart. _____ texture

e. From *Sonata No. 40* by Scarlatti. _____ texture

f. From *Sinfonia No. 2* by J.S. Bach. _____ texture

LESSON 13
CONTRAPUNTAL TECHNIQUES

A **MOTIVE** is a short musical idea that recurs throughout a composition.

A **THEME** is an entire phrase or melody that is the basis of the composition. (A composition may have more than one theme.)

Song of the Traveler, Op. 85, No. 6 by Mendelsson uses this motive:

It is used throughout the music, varied melodically and rhythmically. The beginning of the composition is shown:

REPETITION takes place when the motive is repeated immediately, exactly the way it was the first time it occurred and on the same note.

This example, from *Waltz, Op. 69, No. 1* by Chopin, uses repetition.

SEQUENCE occurs when the motive is repeated immediately on a different note, usually a 2nd or 3rd higher or lower.

This example, from *French Suite No. II: Courante* by J.S. Bach, uses sequence.

IMITATION occurs when the motive is repeated immediately in another voice, such as in the bass clef following a statement of the motive in the treble clef.

This example, from *Invention No. 3* by J.S. Bach, uses imitation.

CANON is a strict copy of an entire melody.*

Dona Nobis Pacem is an example of a canon.

PEDAL POINT or **ORGAN POINT** occurs when there is a sustained or repeated note, usually in the bass (although sometimes in higher voices), which stays for some time while the other voices continue to change harmonies.

This example, from *Invention No. 4* by J.S. Bach, shows the use of pedal or organ point.

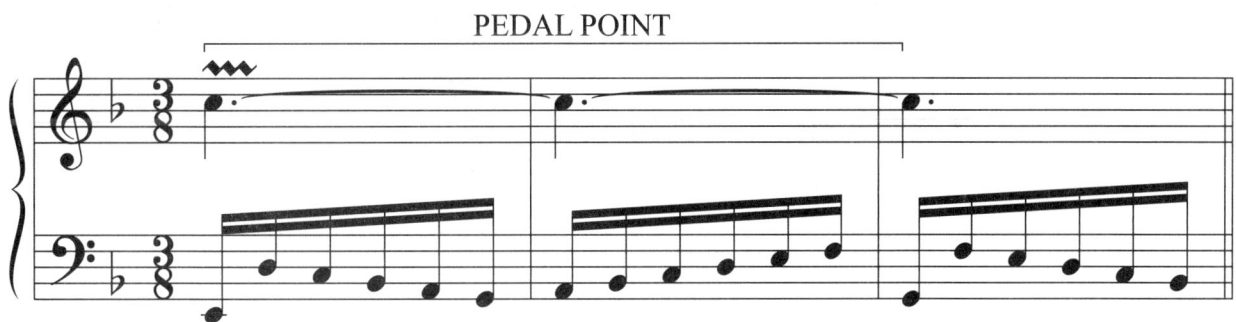

*The term canon may also refer to other types of melodic imitation. Further study is suggested.

AUGMENTATION is the recurrence of a motive or melody, but with the rhythmic values of the notes lengthened. In the following example, the rhythmic values are doubled.

DIMINUTION is the recurrence of a motive or melody, but with the rhythmic values of the notes shortened. In the following example, the rhythmic values are cut in half.

1. For each of the following examples, circle the compositional technique (repetition, imitation, sequence, canon, pedal point, augmentation, or diminution) and write the name of the technique on the line above the music.

   a. From *Aufschwung* by Schumann. _____

   b. From *Sinfonia No. 9* by J.S. Bach. _____

   c. From *Sonata, 1766,* by Haydn. _____

d. _____

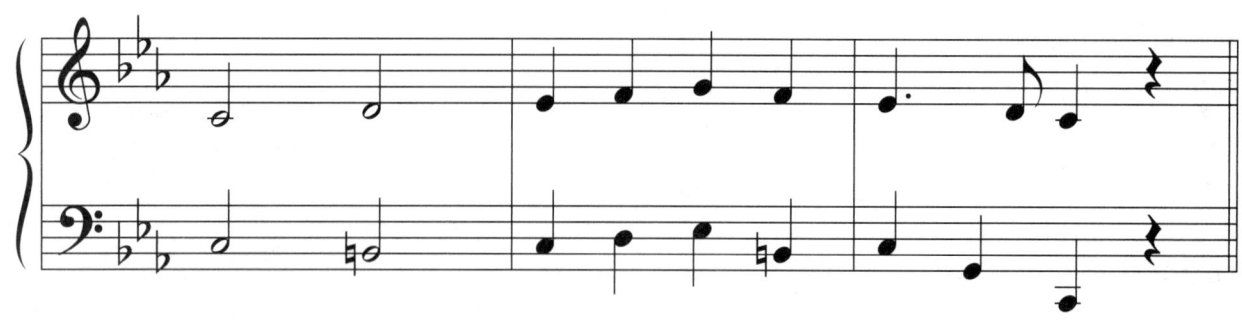

e. From *Sonata Hob. XVI:41,* by Haydn. _____

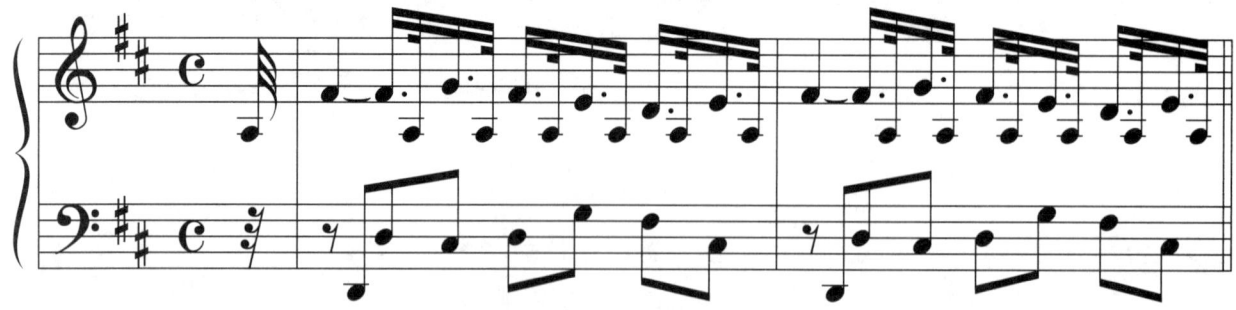

f. From *Sonata, Hob. XVI:41,* by Haydn. _____

g. From *Invention No. 15* by J.S. Bach. _____

h. From *Sonata, XVI:41,* by Haydn. _____

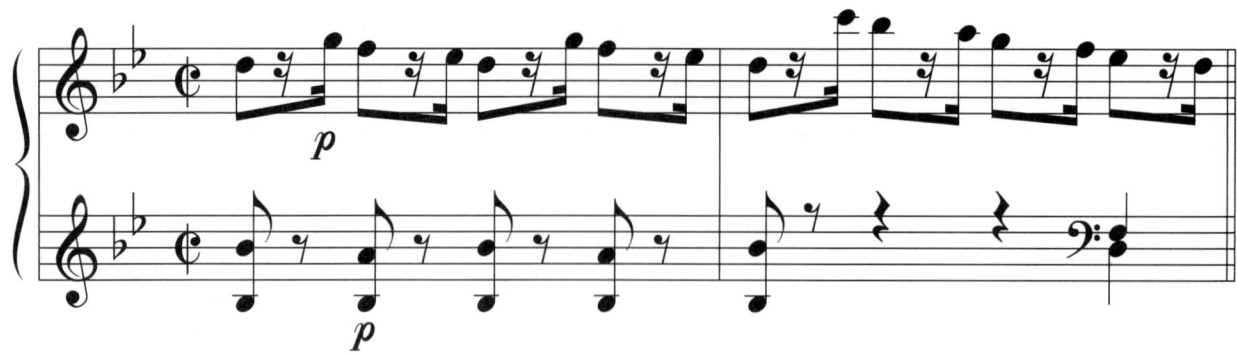

i. From *Sonata, Op. 2, No. 1,* by Beethoven. _____

j. _____

k. _____

1. From *Sinfonia No. 1* by J.S. Bach. _____

110

m. From *Sonata, K. 284* by Mozart. _____

n. From *Sinfonia No. 2* by J.S. Bach. _____

LESSON 14
THE FUGUE

A **FUGUE** is a style of composition in which three or more voices follow one another in an imitative manner.

The **SUBJECT** is the first voice to enter. After the entire subject is heard, the second voice enters, usually at a fifth above or below. While the second voice answers with the transposed subject, the original voice plays a **COUNTERSUBJECT** or other melody against the second voice. Similarly, the third voice enters with the subject, usually at an octave above or below the main subject, while the other two voices continue with their countersubject and/or free counterpoint.

EXAMPLE - THREE VOICE FUGUE		
First Voice	**Second Voice**	**Third Voice**
Subject		
Countersubject	Answer (Subject)	
Free Counterpoint	Countersubject	Subject

The opening section of the fugue, in which all three (or more) voices enter in their entirety, is called the **Exposition.** The fugue then continues with **Episodes,** sections of music that do not contain motives based on the subject or new material. These episodes are alternated with sections that include the entire subject and countersubject. The subject typically returns near the end in the original key, leading up to the closing of the piece.

Terminology used in a fugue:

Exposition: the opening section, containing all voices in their entirety

Answer: the first occurrence of the transposed subject

Subject: the main theme of the fugue.

Countersubject: a different melody from the subject, which occurs at the same time as the subject. In order to be considered a countersubject, this melody must be used again later in the fugue. Not all fugues incude a countersubject.

Episode: a section in which the subject is not present, but instead is made up of new material or motives based on the subject

1. The sections of this fugue (BWV 847) by J.S. Bach are marked. Study them carefully.

2. Mark the sections of the following fugue (BWV 856 by J.S. Bach). Include the exposition, the subject and its answer, each subsequent entrance of the subject and countersubject, and the episodes.

LESSON 15
THE DANCES OF THE BAROQUE SUITE

A **SUITE** consists of several movements. Baroque Suites contain dances, all in the same key.

The Baroque Suite has the standard scheme of:

> **Allemande**
>
> **Courante or Corrente**
>
> **Sarabande**
>
> **Optional Dances** (one or more): Minuet, Bouree, Gavotte, Passepied, Polonaise, Anglaise, Loure, or Air
>
> **Gigue**

ALLEMANDE: a dance in moderate 4/4 time of German origin, with a short upbeat, often using short running figures that are passed through a semi-contrapuntal texture. (Example from *French Suite No. 1* by J.S. Bach.)

119

COURANTE: French dance in moderate 3/2 or 6/4 time, with frequent shifting from one of these to the other (hemiola). The texture is free counterpoint, with a shifting melody. (Example from *French Suite No. 2* by J.S. Bach.)

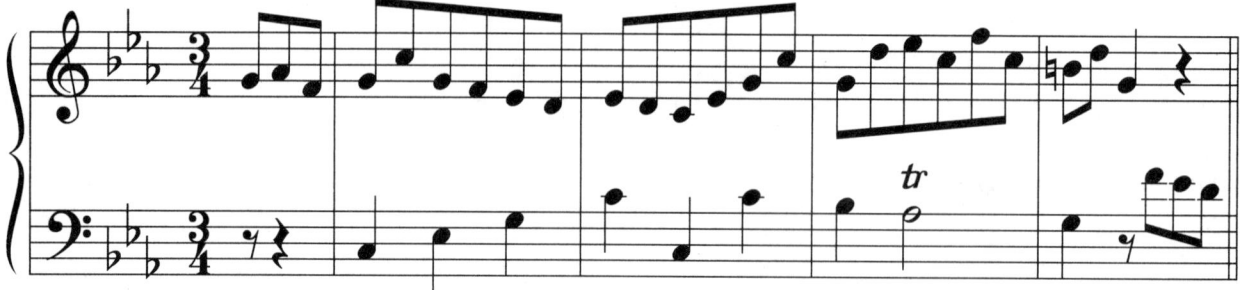

CORRENTE: Italian dance in quick triple meter, with continuous running figures, and homophonic texture. (Example from *Partita No. 1* by J.S. Bach.)

SARABANDE: a dance in slow triple meter and dignified style, often with an accented or long tone on the second beat. It probably originated in Latin America and moved to Spain as a wild dance, but when it arrived in France and England, its style became calm and dignified. (Example from *French Suite No. 2* by J.S. Bach.)

Optional Dances:

Minuet: a French country dance in 3/4 meter. (Example from *French Suite No. 1* by J.S. Bach.)

Bouree: a French dance, usually in quick duple meter with a single upbeat. (Example from *French Suite No. 5* by J.S. Bach.)

Gavotte: a French dance in moderate duple meter, with an upbeat of two quarter notes, and with phrases usually beginning and ending in the middle of the measure. (Example from *French Suite No. 5* by J.S. Bach.)

Passepied: a spirited dance in quick 3/8 or 6/8 meter possibly originating in Brittany, a cultural region in northwestern France. (Example from *French Suite No. 6* by J.S. Bach.)

Polonaise: a Polish dance of stately and festive character, in moderate triple meter. It often contains measures with a short repeated rhythmic motive. (Example from *French Suite No. 6,* by J.S. Bach.)

Anglaise: a dance in fast duple meter, derived from the English country dance. (Example from *French Suite No. 3* by J.S. Bach.)

Loure: from the 16th and 17th century term for bagpipe, this dance is in moderate $\frac{6}{4}$ time, with dotted rhythms and heavy downbeats. (Example from *French Suite No. 5* by J.S. Bach.)

Air: a song, rather than a dance, with melodic characteristics. (Example from *French Suite No. 2* by J.S. Bach.)

GIGUE: Originated from the English Jigs, the **French Gigue** is in compound duple meter ($\frac{6}{8}$, for example), contains dotted rhythms and large intervals (6ths, 7ths), and has fugal texture. The **Italian Giga** is quicker, non-fugal, and has running passages over a harmonic bass. These are less common in Baroque suites than the French Gigue. (Example of *Gigue* from *French Suite No. 6* by J.S. Bach.)

1. Match each of the following dances with its description.

   _____ Courante

   _____ Sarabande

   _____ Allemande

   _____ Corrente

   _____ Gigue

   _____ Optional Dances

   a. Dance in moderate $\frac{4}{4}$ time with a short upbeat, and running figures in a semi-contrapuntal texture.

   b. French dance in $\frac{3}{2}$ or $\frac{6}{4}$ time, using hemiola; texture is free counterpoint with a shifting melody.

   c. Minuet, Bouree, Gavotte, Passepied, Polonaise, Anglaise, Loure, Air.

   d. Dance in slow triple meter and dignified style, often with an accented or long note on the second beat.

   e. Italian dance in quick triple meter, with continuous running figures, and homophonic texture.

   f. Dance in compound duple meter, with dotted rhythms and large intervals.

2. List the dances used in a Baroque Suite in the correct order.

   _____

   _____

   _____

   _____

   _____

LESSON 16
SONATA FORM

A **SONATA** is a composition for piano or another instrument which has several separate sections called **movements**, one or more of which is in sonata form.

The normal scheme for the movements of a sonata are:

Allegro: Sonata form (sometimes called Sonata Allegro form)

Adagio: Binary (two-part, *e.g.* AB) or Ternary (three-part, *e.g.* ABA) form, in a key different but closely related to that of the first movement such as the dominant or relative minor

Scherzo or Minuet: Ternary form (Scherzo and Trio or Minuet and Trio), in the same key as the first movement.

Allegro (or Presto): Rondo form (*e.g.* ABACABA) or Variations, in the same key as the first movement.

This scheme is not always followed. Often there are fewer than four movements (in which case it is usually the Scherzo/Minuet movement that is missing), or a Sonata may begin with a slow movement rather than a fast movement.

SONATA FORM

EXPOSITION		DEVELOPMENT	RECAPITULATION	
Theme 1 (Tonic key)	**Theme 2** (Dominant or related key)	Motives based on Themes 1 and 2 are developed in various ways	**Theme 1** (Tonic key)	**Theme 2** (Tonic key)

Typically, the exposition is repeated, then the development and recapitulation are repeated.

The first movement of *Sonata, XVI:27* by Haydn, is given below. The sections and themes (with their keys) are marked. Study this sonata.

The second movement of this sonata is a Minuet and Trio in the key of G Major (Tonic).

The third movement is a Rondo in the key of G Major (Tonic). (Music for the second and third movements are not included in this workbook.)

EXPOSITION

128

DEVELOPMENT

(Various keys)

RECAPITULATION
Theme 1 (G Major, I)

Theme 2 (G Major, I)

1. Mark the sections of this *Sonata, K. 283,* by Mozart. Include the Exposition, Development, Recapitulation, Themes 1 and 2, and their keys (letter names and Roman numerals).

LESSON 17
SIGNS AND TERMS

The following performance terms may appear in music you are studying.

a tempo: return to the original tempo

 accent: play the note louder than the others

accelerando: accelerate; gradually faster

adagio: slowly

allargando: broadening; gradually slower

allegro: fast or quick, cheerfully, merrily

allegretto: slighly slower than *allegro;* faster than *andante*

andante: a moderate walking tempo

andantino: slightly faster than *andante;* some composers use it to mean slower than *andante*

animato: animated; with spirit

 *appoggiatura:* used mainly in music of the Classical Period, play the first note as half the value of the second note (other interpretations are possible; further study is recommended):

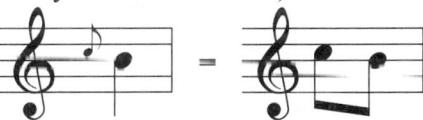

articulation: the manner in which notes are executed, including but not limited to *staccato* and *legato*.

arpeggio: a broken chord:

atonality: no specific key or tonality

bitonality: the use of two different keys at the same time

canon: a strict form of contrapuntal writing in which each voice exactly imitates the melody of the first voice.

cantabile: in a singing style

coda: an extended ending

codetta: a short coda, or a short section of music that connects two other sections but is not part of either

con: with.

con brio: with vigor or spirit, with brilliance

con fuoco: with fire or fury

con moto: with motion

crescendo (cresc.): gradually louder

D.C. al fine: go back to the beginning and play to *fine*

𝒫𝑒𝒹. ✽ or |⎯⎯⎯| **damper pedal:** press the pedal located on the right

decrescendo (decresc.) or diminuendo (dim.): gradually softer

dolce: sweetly

doloroso: sadly; sorrowfully

double flat: two flats placed before a note, indicating to lower the note a whole step

B double flat is the same pitch as A

double sharp: the symbol 𝄪 placed before a note, indicating to raise the note a whole step

G double sharp is the same pitch as A

dynamics: letters or symbols which tell how loudly or softly to play the music

enharmonic: two different names for the same pitch, such as C♯ and D♭

espressivo: expressively

fine: the end

f *forte:* loud

ff *fortissimo:* very loud

fff *fortississimo:* very, very loud

fp *forte-piano:* loud followed immediately by soft

⌢ *fermata:* hold the note longer than its value

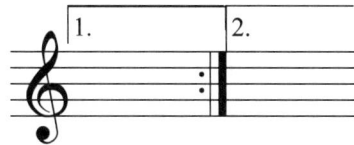 **First and Second Ending:** play the music with the first ending (under the 1.), then repeat the music; the second time through, skip the first ending and play the second ending (under the 2.)

giocoso: merrily, with humor

gracioso: gracefully

largo: very slowly

legato: play smoothly; connect the notes

leggiero: lightly, delicately

lento: slowly

m.d.: *mano destra;* use the right hand

m.s.: *mano sinistra;* use the left hand

marcato: stressed, marked

meno: less

meno mosso: less motion; slower

mf *mezzo forte*: medium loud

mp *mezzo piano:* medium soft

moderato: a moderate or medium tempo

molto: much; very

 **mordent:** an ornament in which the written note is played, followed by the note below the written note and the written note again:

 **octave sign (8va):** play the notes an octave higher (or lower if below the notes) than where they are written

opus: a word used to indicate the chronological order in which a composer's music was written

ostinato: a persistently repeated pattern:  or

parallel Major/minor: major and minor keys with the same letter names, such as C Major and c minor

p *piano:* soft

pp *pianissimo:* very soft

ppp *pianississimo:* very, very soft

pesante: heavily

phrase: a musical sentence, often but not always four measures long

piu: more

piu mosso: more motion; faster

poco: little

polytonality: the use of several different keys at the same time

presto: very fast

rallentando (rall.): gradually slower

relative Major and minor: Major and minor keys which have the same key signature

‖: :‖ **repeat sign:** repeat the previous sections of music; go back to the nearest repeat sign, or to the beginning if there is none

ritardando (ritard., rit.,): gradually slower

ritenuto (riten.): immediately slower

robusto: robustly, boldly

rubato: the practice of varying the rhythm of a phrase by slowing or rushing the tempo, making up the changed time elsewhere in the phrase; "robbed time"

scherzando: playfully, jokingly

sempre: Always.

senza: Without.

 **sforzando:** a sudden, sharp accent

smorzando: dying away

simile: continue in the same style

slur: curved line indicating to play *legato*

spiritoso: spirited; with spirit

sostenuto: sustained

sotto voce: in a low voice

 staccato: play crisply or detached

subito: suddenly; at once

syncopation: a momentary contradiction of the meter or pulse, often by changing strong and weak beats within a measure, for example:

tempo: the speed at which to play the music.

tenuto: hold the note for its full value; may also mean to stress the note

tie: hold the second note; do not play it

toccata: a virtuoso piece common during the Baroque Period, written in free style with many scales and rapid passages

tranquillo: tranquilly, peacefully, calmly

tre corde (t.c.): release the *una corda* pedal (soft pedal; left pedal)

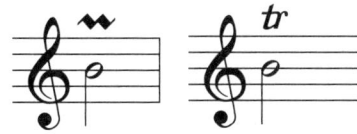 **trill:** an ornament in which the written note is alternated with the note above (trills may be interpreted differently):

Baroque or Classical Period: begin on the note above the written note.

Romantic Period: begin on the written note.

 **trill with prefix:** a trill performed with an added beginning from above or below

 **turn:** an ornament in which the written note is surrounded by its upper and lower neighbors:

una corda (u.c.): press the left or soft pedal

vivace: quick, lively

vivo: brisk, lively

...etto: a suffix meaning little or less than, such as *allegretto* for a little slower than *allegro*

...ino: a suffix meaning little or less than, such as *andantino* for a little faster than *andante*

1. Match each of the following terms or symbols with its definition.

_____ *ff* a. *mezzo piano:* medium soft

_____ *fff* b. *pianissimo:* very soft

_____ *sfz* c. *piano:* soft

_____ *f* d. *fortissimo:* very loud

_____ *pp* e. *mezzo forte:* medium loud

_____ 8*va* f. symbols that indicate loud or soft

_____ dynamics g. *forte:* loud

_____ *mp* h. play one octave higher

_____ *mf* i. *fortississimo:* very, very loud

_____ *ppp* j. *sforzando:* a sudden, sharp accent

_____ *p* k. *pianississimo:* very, very soft

2. Match each of the following terms or symbols with its definition.

_____ ||: :||

_____ [fermata/1st-2nd ending symbol]

_____ [staccato note]

_____ legato

_____ [slur over four notes]

a. connect the notes, play smoothly

b. repeat sign: repeat the music

c. *staccato:* crisply or detached

d. slur, play *legato*

e. *fermata:* hold the note longer than its value

f. first and second ending

3. Match each of the following terms or symbols with its definition.

_____ [accented note]

_____ Ped. ✽ |_____|

_____ phrase

_____ [tenuto note]

_____ D. C. al fine

_____ *ritardando (rit.)*

_____ *a tempo*

a. use the damper pedal (the pedal on the right)

b. a musical sentence, often but not always four measures long

c. hold the note for its full value; may mean to stress the note

d. accent: play the note louder than the others

e. gradually slower

f. return to the original tempo

g. go back to the beginning and play to *fine*

4. Match each of the following terms or symbols with its definition.

_____ *allegro*   a. walking tempo

_____ *andante*   b. gradually louder

_____ *moderato*   c. slow down gradually

_____ *vivace*   d. gradually softer

_____ >   e. slowly

_____ <   f. a moderate or medium tempo

_____ *adagio*   g. quick or lively

_____ *lento*   h. with brilliance

_____ *rallentando (rall.)*   i. fast, quick, cheerfully, merrily

_____ *con brio*   j. slowly

5. Match each of the following terms or symbols with its definition.

_____ *fp*   a. sadly, sorrowfully

_____ *scherzando*   b. boldly, robustly

_____ *doloroso*   c. more

_____ *opus*   d. heavily

_____ *robusto*   e. sustained

_____ *piu*   f. playfully, jokingly

_____ *pesante*   g. system of classifying a composer's works chronologically

_____ *sostenuto*   h. loud, followed immediately by soft

6. Match each of the following terms or symbols with its definition.

_____ andantino

_____ con moto

_____ dolce

_____ [appoggiatura notation]

_____ accelerando

_____ [trill tr notation]

_____ una corda (u.c.)

_____ cantabile

_____ molto

_____ [mordent notation]

_____ [turn notation]

_____ codetta

_____ poco

_____ tre corde (t.c.)

_____ spiritoso

_____ [trill with prefix notation]

_____ coda

_____ sempre

_____ [trill with prefix notation]

a. trill: [notation]

b. gradually faster

c. trill with prefix: [notation]

d. use soft pedal (left pedal)

e. slightly faster than *andante*

f. sweetly

g. with motion

h. with spirit

i. little

j. much, greatly

k. a short coda, or a short section of music that connects two other sections but is not part of either

l. release the soft pedal (left pedal)

m. trill with prefix: [notation]

n. in a singing style

o. mordent: [notation]

p. an extended ending

q. *appoggiatura:* [notation]

r. always

s. turn: [notation]

7. Match each of the following terms or symbols with its definition.

_____ *presto* a. expressively

_____ *vivo* b. without

_____ *espressivo* c. suddenly; at once

_____ *leggiero* d. very fast

_____ *senza* e. stressed; marked

_____ *marcato* f. brisk, lively

_____ *subito* g. continue in the same style

_____ *simile* h. lightly; delicately

8. Match each of the following terms or symbols with its definition.

_____ *largo* a. animated; with spirit

_____ *giocoso* b. gracefully

_____ *animato* c. with fire

_____ bitonality d. no specific key or tonality

_____ *allegretto* e. peacefully; calmly; tranquilly

_____ *grazioso* f. merrily; with humor

_____ *con fuoco* g. the use of two different keys at the same time

_____ atonality h. slightly slower than *allegro*

_____ polytonality i. very slowly

_____ *tranquillo* j. the use of several different keys at the same time

9. Match each of the following terms or symbols with its definition.

_____ *allargando*   a. two names for the same pitch
_____ *...etto*   b. broadening, gradually slower
_____ *...ino*   c. suffix meaning "little"
_____ *meno*   d. less motion
_____ canon   e. less
_____ *ritenuto (riten.)*   f. momentary contradiction of beat, often by using strong notes on weak beats
_____ enharmonic
_____ parallel Major and minor   g. Major and minor keys with the same key signature
_____ relative Major and minor   h. immediately slower
_____ *meno mosso*   i. suffix meaning "little"
_____ *piu mosso*   j. a strict form of contrapuntal writing in which each voice exactly imitates the melody of the first voice
_____ syncopation   k. more motion
_____ exposition   l. Major and minor keys with the same letter names
_____ development   m. composition made up of separate but related pieces
_____ recapitulation   n. the middle section of Sonata form
_____ fugue   o. the third section of Sonata form
_____ suite   p. a style of composition in which the subject (theme) is imitated by other voices
                            q. the first section of Sonata form

10. Match each of the following terms or symbols with its definition.

_____ *arpeggio*   a. ✖ raise the note a whole step
_____ *ostinato*   b. a broken chord
_____ double sharp   c. fluctuation of the tempo
_____ double flat   d. in a low voice
_____ *m.d.*   e. use left hand
_____ *m.s.*   f. dying away
_____ *rubato*   g. a persistently repeated pattern
_____ *smorzando*   h. use right hand
_____ *sotto voce*   i. lower the note a whole step
_____ *toccata*   j. Baroque virtuoso piece, free style, scales, rapid passages

LESSON 18
TRANSPOSITION

TRANSPOSITION occurs when music is played or written in a key that is different from the original.

The first version of *Frere Jacques* below (Example A) is in the key of C Major. The second version (Example B) is in G Major. The song has been transposed from C Major to G Major.

Notice how the intervals remain the same in both versions. The melody sounds the same but is higher in pitch.

EXAMPLE A: FRERE JACQUES in the key of C Major

EXAMPLE B: FRERE JACQUES in the key of G Major

TRANSPOSING A MELODY: METHOD 1

1. Look at the first note of the original melody and determine its scale degree.

   G Major: 3rd (mediant)

2. Notate the first note of the melody in the new key, on the appropriate scale degree. Use the correct rhythm.

   D Major: 3rd (mediant)

3. Name the intervals in the original melody.

   m2 M2 P5 P4 M3 m2

4. Continue the melody in the new key using the same intervals and directions (up or down) that appear in the original melody. Use the correct rhythm.

   m2 M2 P5 P4 M3 m2

TRANSPOSING A MELODY: METHOD 2

1. Compare the original key with the new key. Determine the interval between the original key and the new key.

G Major to D Major: Up a Perfect 5th

2. Move each note of the original melody the distance of that interval.

G becomes D
A becomes E
B becomes F♯
C becomes G
D becomes A
E becomes B
F♯ becomes C♯

3. Notate the melody in the new key using the correct rhythm and directions.

The following example, from *Mary had a Little Lamb,* is transposed from C Major to G Major.

   Method 1: Each interval is marked, and the transposition is based on the original intervals.

   Method 2: Each note has been raised a Perfect 5th.

MARY HAD A LITTLE LAMB in C Major

MARY HAD A LITTLE LAMB in G Major

1. Transpose the following example to the key of E♭ Major. Notate the transposition on the blank staff below the excerpt.

Haydn: *Allegro Scherzando*

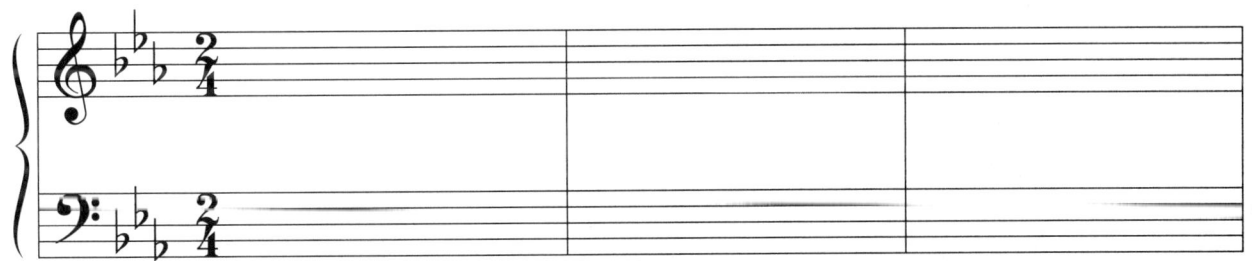

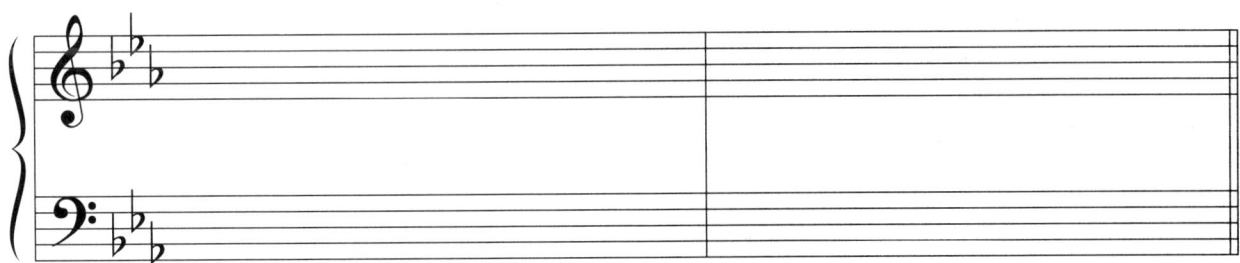

2. Transpose the following example to the key of b minor. Notate the transposition on the blank staff below the excerpt.

J.S. Bach: *Polonaise*

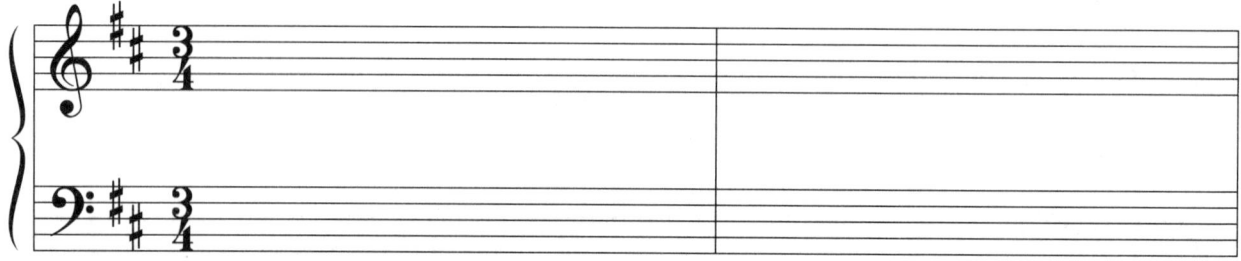

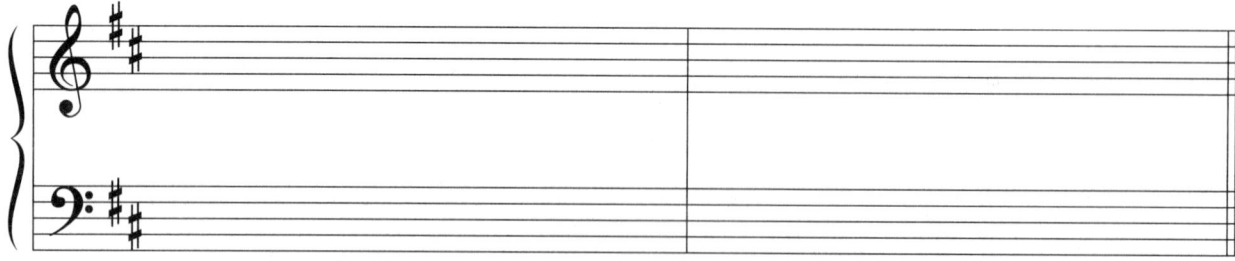

LESSON 19
THE FOUR PERIODS OF MUSIC HISTORY
THE BAROQUE PERIOD
CORELLI, PURCELL, AND RAMEAU

The history of music since 1600 is divided into four periods (dates are approximate):

Baroque: 1600-1750

Classical: 1750-1830

Romantic: 1830-1900

20th & 21st Centuries: 1900-present

(Currently, there is not a definitive name for stylistic periods of the 20th and 21st Centuries. It is sometimes called the "Contemporary Period," "Modern," or "Post-Common Practice." It may also be divided into two groups: the 20th Century (1900-1999), and the Contemporary Period (2000-Present).

Music of the **BAROQUE PERIOD** (appx. 1600-1750) is characterized by the following:

a. **Polyphonic Texture:** Two or more separate voices are interwoven to create the music. The melodies are passed between the parts, and the parts are of equal importance.

b. **Use of Ornamentation:** Composers included many trills, mordents, and other ornaments in their music. It was the performer's responsibility to know how to play the ornaments correctly. Performers could also add their own ornaments at appropriate places in the music.

c. **Improvisation:** Not only did music of the Baroque Period contain many ornaments, the performer was also free to improvise sections of the music. This not only included adding the ornaments mentioned above, but also playing **Cadenzas**, entire sections of music that the performer created, often after a cadence in the music.

Another type of improvisation in Baroque music included the use of **Figured Bass.** The performer was given an outline of the chord progression of a composition. The performer improvised using the harmonies specified by the figured bass.

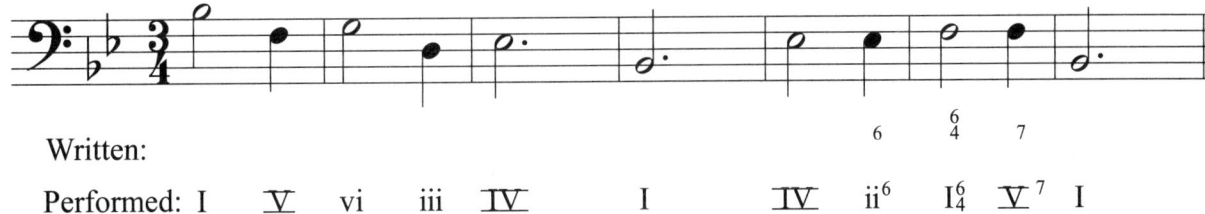

Written:

Performed: I   V   vi   iii   IV   I   IV   ii^6 I$^6_4$ V^7 I

152

d. **Dance Suite:** a composition which contains many different dances, all in the same key. (See Lssson 15.)

e. Most keyboard music of the Baroque Period was written for the **harpsichord, clavichord,** and **organ**. The piano was not invented until fairly late in the Baroque Period. (The piano was invented sometime around 1700 by Bartolomeo Cristofori, but did not gain widespread use until several years later.)

f. **Terraced Dynamics:** Since much of the keyboard music from the Baroque Period was written for the harpsichord, which does not have the capability of making *crescendos* or *diminuendos,* performers used terraced dynamics. This takes place when the dynamics increase or decrease suddenly: *p mp mf f*, rather than gradually. (This type of dynamic contrast is most prevelant in keyboard music of the period. Other instruments, such as the violin, did create true *crescendos* and *decrescendos* during the Baroque Period.)

This example, from *Short Prelude No. 7* by J.S. Bach, shows these characteristics: Polyphonic texture and terraced dynamics.

ARCANGELO CORELLI

* Born in Italy, 1653-1713

* Violinist and composer

* Came from wealthy family; took violin lessons and performed as a young boy

* Worked as director of music to Cardinal Pamphili, and later to Cardinal Pietro Ottoboni

* Wrote several volumes of chamber music, including trio sonatas and solo violin sonatas

* Most famous work is *Christmas Concerto*

* Compositional style includes key changes and dissonance, which were innovative for his time

HENRY PURCELL

* Born in England, 1659-1695

* Composed songs at age eight

* Sang in boys choir at Chapel Royal

* When voice changed, worked taking care of instruments and copying music for Westminster Abby

* Eventually hired as organist for Westminster Abbey

* In 1682 became organist of Chapel Royal

* Wrote music for the coronation of James II and the funeral of Queen Mary

* Works include instrumental music, choral anthems, four operas, longer choral works with orchestra

* Music was neglected after his death until the late 1800's

JEAN PHILLIP RAMEAU

* Born in France, 1683-1764

* Son of an organist

* Went to Italy at age eighteen to study music

* Worked as organist in Avignon, Clermont, Paris, Notre Dame, and Clermont Cathedral, France

* Returned to Paris in 1722, where he remained

* Works include harpsichord works, operas, ballets, and other types of stage works, and instrumental chamber music

* Theoretical works include *Traied de l'harmonie, Nouveau systeme de musique;* was an innovator in the development of Major and minor harmony and bass movement

Some other well known Baroque composers are:

J.S. Bach, born in Germany, 1685-1750

Girolamo Frescobaldi, born in Italy, 1583-1643

G.F. Handel, born in Germany, 1685-1760

Johann Philipp Kirnberger, born in Germany, 1721-1783

Domenico Scarlatti, born in Italy, 1685-1757

Antonio Soler, born in Spain, 1729-1783

Georg Philipp Telemann, born in Germany, 1681-1767

Antonio Vivaldi, born in Italy, 1678-1741

1. Name the four periods of music history and give their dates.

    _____   _____

    _____   _____

    _____   _____

    _____   _____

2. List six characteristics of Baroque music and describe each.

    a. _____

    _____

    b. _____

    _____

    c. _____

    _____

    d. _____

    _____

e. _____

f. _____

3. Complete the following information about each of these composers.

a. **Arcangelo Corelli**

Dates of birth and death: _____

Historical period: _____

Country of birth: _____

Positions held: _____

_____

Types of compositions: _____

_____

Compositional Style: _____

_____

b. **Henry Purcell**

Dates of birth and death: _____

Historical period: _____

Country of birth: _____

Positions held: _____

_____

Types of works: _____

_____

c. **Jean Phillip Rameau**

Dates of birth and death: _____

Historical period: _____

Country of birth: _____

Positions held: _____

_____

Types of compositions: _____

_____

Theoretical works: _____

4. Name eight other Baroque composers, their places of birth, and their dates of birth and death.

_____	_____	_____
_____	_____	_____
_____	_____	_____
_____	_____	_____
_____	_____	_____
_____	_____	_____
_____	_____	_____
_____	_____	_____

LESSON 20
THE CLASSICAL PERIOD
BEETHOVEN, HAYDN, AND MOZART

The **CLASSICAL PERIOD** of music took place from approximately 1750-1830. Music from the Classical Period includes the following characteristics:

a. **Homophonic Texture:** Much of the music of the Classical Period has an obvious melody with accompaniment.

b. **Cadence points usually obvious:** Quite often, the harmonic structure of Classical music is clear, and the cadences are obvious, both harmonically and by the use of rests at the ends of sections.

c. **Alberti Bass:** A common type of accompaniment for the left hand part of piano music from the Classical Period is Alberti Bass, a broken chord accompaniment with the specific pattern of **low-high-middle-high:**

ALBERTI BASS

d. **Sonata and Sonatina forms** developed: see Lesson 16 for a detailed explanation of Sonata Form.

This example, from *Sonatina, Op. 36, No. 3* by Clementi, shows these characteristics: Homophonic texture, clear melody and harmony, and use of rests.

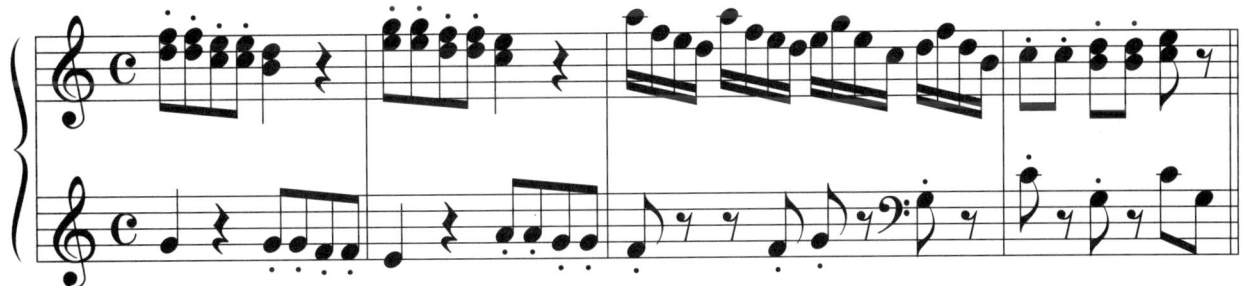

LUDWIG VAN BEETHOVEN

* Born in Bonn, Germany, 1770-1827

* Went to Vienna in 1790 to work as a professional pianist and teacher

* Known for improvising during his performances

* Studied with Haydn

* Made his living as a professional composer (via commissions, dedications to royalty, etc.)

* Much of his music was influenced by events in the French Revolution

* Lost his hearing completely, yet continued composing

* Works include string quartets, piano concertos, piano sonatas, symphonies, works for solo instruments, piano trios

* Helped bridge the gap between the Classical Period and the Romantic Period with his style

FRANZ JOSEF HAYDN

* Born in Austria, 1732-1809

* Studied at the Vienna Choir School

* Was dismissed from the school when he played a practical joke on a fellow student

* Began his career as a teacher and professional singer

* Was later hired to a permanent position as music director to Prince Esterhazy

* Did some traveling to London to compose and direct

* Works include piano sonatas, operas, string quartets, over 100 symphonies, giving him the nickname "Father of the Symphony" or "Papa Haydn"

* Developed the standard four-movement format for symphonies and Sonata form

WOLFGANG AMADEUS MOZART

* Born in Austria, 1756-1791

* Child prodigy; performed and traveled throughout Europe with his father Leopold and sister Nanerl

* Began improvising and composing before age five

* Traveled extensively throughout Europe as a young man, composing and performing

* Worked as music director for the Archbishop of Salzburg, but conflicts with his employer caused this position to cease

* Went to Vienna to live and work as a professional composer and teacher

* Lived much of his life in poverty

* Works include piano sonatas, piano concertos, operas, symphonies, sonatas and concertos for other instruments, a Requiem for choir and orchestra

Other composers of the Classical period include:

Muzio Clementi, born in Italy, 1752-1832

Carl Czerny, born in Austria, 1791-1857

Anton Diabelli, born in Austria, 1781-1858

Frederich Kuhlau, born in Germany, 1786-1832

1. List four characteristics of music from the Classical Period and describe each.

a. _____

_____

_____

b. _____

_____

_____

c. _____

_____

_____

d. _____

_____

_____

2. Complete the following information about each of these composers.

a. **Ludwig van Beethoven**

Dates of birth and death: _____

Historical period: _____

Country of birth: _____

Types of compositions: _____

_____

Music influenced by: _____

_____

Studied with: _____

b. **Franz Josef Haydn**

Dates of birth and death: _____

Historical period: _____

Country of birth: _____

Education: _____

Musical form which he developed: _____

Positions held: _____

_____

Types of works: _____

_____

c. Wolfgang Amadeus Mozart

Dates of birth and death: _____

Historical period: _____

Country of birth: _____

Childhood: _____

Types of compositions: _____

_____

Positions held: _____

_____

3. Name four other Classical composers, their places of birth, and their dates of birth and death.

_____	_____	_____
_____	_____	_____
_____	_____	_____
_____	_____	_____

LESSON 21
THE ROMANTIC PERIOD
BRAHMS, LISZT, AND TCHAIKOVSKY

The **ROMANTIC PERIOD** was from approximately 1830-1900. Music of the Romantic Period is the most popular of the four periods of music history. Some characteristics of this music are:

a. **Programme Music (Program Music):** Much of the music of the Romantic period was written about things, people, places, or feelings. The titles in music of the period reflect the mood of the piece (such as *Curious Story* by Heller, *Blindman's Buff* by Schumann, or *Valse Melancolique* by Rebikoff).

b. **Harmonies more complicated:** Composers began to add more colorful notes to their chords, using more chromaticism, and straying from the tonal scale.

c. **Lyric melodies:** Many of the melodies in music of the Romantic period are lovely, singing melodies that have become favorites among music lovers.

d. **Rhythms more complicated:** Music of the Romantic period contains many syncopated rhythms, complicated sixteenth note patterns, dotted rhythms, triplets, cross rhythms (two against three), etc.

This example, from *Reaper's Song* by Schumann, shows these characteristics: A descriptive title, more complex chords, more complicated rhythms, lyric melody.

JOHANNES BRAHMS

* Born in Germany, 1833-1897

* Son of a bass player

* Supported himself as a teenager by playing piano in taverns

* Toured Europe with the violinist Remenyi in 1853

* After the tour, visited Liszt and Schumann, who helped launch his career

* After Schumann's death, remained close friends with his wife Clara

* Worked as musical director at a small court in Detmold, and later as conductor of the Singakademie in Vienna

* After the success of his German Requiem in 1868, he made a living as a professional composer and performer

* Works include two piano concertos, sonatas, piano quartets and quintets, the Requiem, other choral works, symphonies, short piano pieces, clarinet sonatas

* Enjoyed fame during his lifetime, and was offered honorary degrees from Cambridge and Breslau

FRANZ LISZT

* Born in Hungary, 1811-1886

* Son of an amateur musician

* As a boy, received financial assistance based on talent which allowed him to study with Czerny and Salieri

* Child prodigy; traveled and performed

* As an adult, had a reputation as the greatest pianist ever, and extremely popular

* In 1848 became Kappelmeister Extraordinary in Weimar

* Music inspired by his homeland (Hungary)

* Works include many piano works: sonatas, *Hungarian Rhapsodies, Consolations,* ballades, polonaises, *Transcendental Etudes,* and more. Also wrote piano concertos, symphonic poems, songs, transcriptions of works by Berlioz, Beethoven, Schubert, and others, choral works, including oratorios

PETER ILYICH TCHAIKOVSKY

* Born in Russia, 1840-1893

* Attended the St. Petersburg School of Jurisprudence from ages 10-19

* Studied composition with Anton Rubinstein

* Taught at Moscow Conservatory from 1866-1878

* Wrote textbooks, including *Guide to the Practical Study of Harmony*

* Works include operas, symphonic poems, ballets (*Swan Lake* and *The Nutcracker* being the most famous), piano concertos, symphonies, violin concerto

* Influenced by the folk music with which he was raised

Other Romantic composers include:

Frederick Chopin, born in Poland, 1810-1849

Antonin Dvorák, born in Czechoslovakia, 1841-1904

John Field, born in Ireland, 1782-1837

Edvard Grieg, born in Norway, 1843-1907

Stephen Heller, born in Hungary, 1813-1888

Felix Bartholdy-Mendelssohn, born in Germany, 1809-1847

Franz Schubert, born in Austria, 1797-1828

Robert Schumann, born in Germany, 1810-1856

1. List four characteristics of music from the Romantic Period and describe each.

   a. _____

   _____

   _____

   b. _____

   _____

   _____

   c. _____

   _____

   _____

   d. _____

   _____

   _____

2. Complete the following information about each of these composers.

a. Johannes Brahms

Dates of birth and death: _____

Historical Period: _____

Country of birth: _____

Works: _____

_____

_____

Composers with whom associated: _____

_____

b. Franz Liszt

Dates of birth and death: _____

Historical Period: _____

Country of birth: _____

Childhood: _____

_____

Positions held: _____

_____

Types of compositions: _____

_____

_____

Inspired by: _____

c. **Peter Ilyich Tchaikovsky**

Dates of birth and death: _____

Historical Period: _____

Country of birth: _____

Education: _____

Positions held: _____

_____

Types of compositions: _____

_____

_____

Other contributions to music: _____

_____

Influenced by: _____

3. Name eight other Romantic composers, their places of birth, and their dates of birth and death.

LESSON 22
IMPRESSIONISM IN MUSIC
DEBUSSY, RAVEL, GRIFFES

IMPRESSIONISM is sometimes used to describe music of a few late 19th and early 20th century composers, particularly Debussy and Ravel. The term Impressionism is borrowed from the art movement that included the works of Monet, Degas, and Renoir whose images are blurred, creating an impression rather than a clear picture.

Impressionistic music includes unclear tonalities, non-metric rhythms, and tends to flow in musically blurred images. Musical components include, but are not limited to:

* whole tone scales
* augmented triads
* ostinato figures

* pentatonic (five-note) scales, for example:

* parallel intervals and chords (moving in the
  same direction without changing intervals):

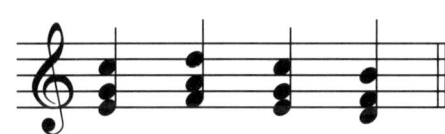

This example, from the Prelude *Voiles* by Debussy, shows use of the whole tone scale, parallel thirds, is musically "blurred," and contains an ostinato figure.

CLAUDE DEBUSSY

* Born in France, 1862-1918

* Received no formal music training until 1871 when he entered the Paris Conservatory

* Studied composition with Guiraud

* Won the Prix de Rome in 1884 with his cantata *L'enfant prodigue*

* Made his living as a professional composer and conductor

* Works include piano preludes and etudes, opera, orchestral works, *Children's Corner* suite for piano

* Style of music is freer than conventional Romantic style, with emphasis on color and timber rather than form and harmony

MAURICE RAVEL

* Born in France, 1875-1937

* Raised in Paris; attended Paris Conservatory

* His well known work *Bolero* for orchestra uses a single melody which is repeated over and over, building from a single instrument to the full orchestra in a crescendo of color

* Other works include *Pavane for a Dead Princess* for piano (later scored for orchestra), *Miroirs* for piano, *Scheherazade* for orchestra, ballet *Daphnes and Chloe*

* Well known for his beautiful orchestrations of his own and others' works

CHARLES TOMLINSON GRIFFES

* Born in U.S.A., 1884-1920

* Studied piano with Mary Selna Broughton, who financed his later studies in Berlin at the Stern Conservatory

* Returned to the U.S. in 1907, and taught at the Hackley School in Tarrytown, New York

* Early compositions are more structured; later works show the influences of the Impressionistic movement

* Also influenced by traditional Japanese songs

* Works include songs, chamber music, stage works, a piano sonata, several short pieces for piano

1. Name some of the characteristics of Impressionistic music.

_____

_____

_____

_____

2. Complete the following information about each of these composers.

a. **Claude Debussy**

Dates of birth and death: _____

Historical Period: _____

Country of birth: _____

Education: _____

Made living as: _____

Types of compositions: _____

_____

_____

b. Maurice Ravel

Dates of birth and death: _____

Historical Period: _____

Country of birth: _____

Education: _____

Types of compositions: _____

_____

_____

Besides compositions, known for: _____

c. Charles Tomlinson Griffes

Dates of birth and death: _____

Historical Period: _____

Country of birth: _____

Education: _____

Positions held: _____

_____

Types of compositions: _____

_____

_____

Influenced by: _____

LESSON 23
THE 20th and 21st CENTURIES
COPLAND, IVES, GERSHWIN

Many changes have taken place in the way music sounds during the **20th and 21st Centuries (1900-present).**

a. **Major and minor tonalities avoided:** Music is often written outside of Major or minor tonalities; non-tonal notes are added to chords.

b. **Quartal Harmony:** chords based on the interval of a fourth:

QUARTAL HARMONY

c. **Bitonality:** the use of two different keys at the same time:

BITONALITY

d. **Polytonality:** the use of many different keys at the same time:

POLYTONALITY

e. **Atonality:** No specific key used.

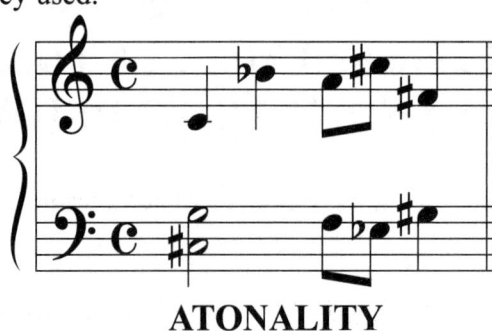

ATONALITY

f. **Irregular and changing meters:** Composers often use uncommon time signatures such as $\frac{5}{4}$ or $\frac{7}{4}$, or change the time signature during the course of the music (complex meter).

g. **Polyphonic texture:** This texture is often used, with the harmonies becoming the result of the interweaving of the melodic lines.

h. **Neo-Classic writing:** Composers often write Sonatas, Sonatinas, or other forms which were common during the Classical Period.

i. **Serial* or Twelve-Tone Music:** a style of writing in which the twelve tones of the chromatic scale are arranged in a fixed style, or series; the entire piece will then be based on the intervals of the series.

The **Prime** is the original series, usually presented first in the composition.

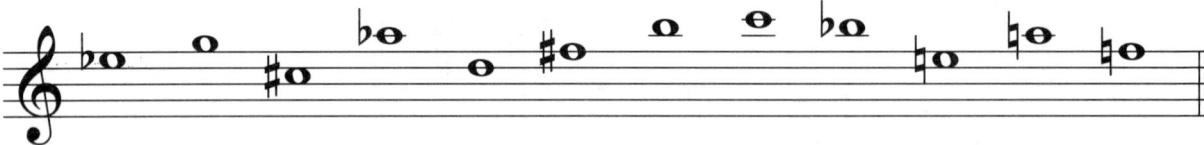

The **Inversion** is created by inverting all the intervals of the prime (for example, P4 up becomes P4 down).

The **Retrograde** is created by reversing the prime.

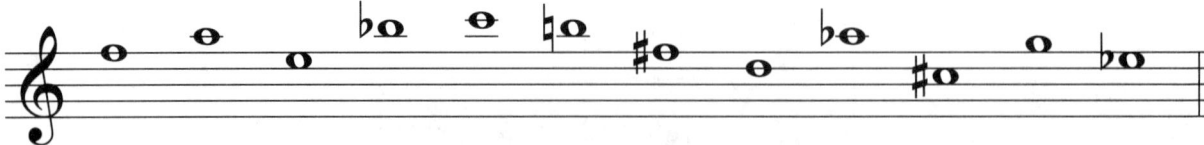

The **Retrograde Inversion** is created by inverting the intervals of the retrograde.

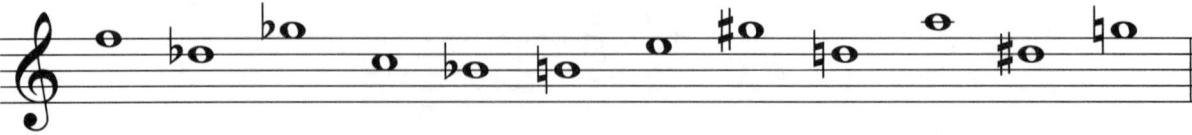

*Serialism may be more broadly defined as a method of composition using a series of pitches, rhythms, dynamics, or other music elements that are repeated over and over, regardless of whether all twelve tones are used.

The following example includes polyphonic texture, changing (complex) meter, and avoidance of Major and minor tonalities.

AARON COPLAND

* Born in U.S.A., 1900-1990

* Began piano study at age thirteen

* Taught at New School for Social Research in New York from 1927-1937

* Taught composition at Tanglewood (1940-1965)

* Early works show use of neo-classic style combined with jazz elements

* Later works show a distinctively American style, influenced by folk music

* Famous works include *El Salon Mexico,* the ballets *Billy the Kid, Rodeo,* and *Appalachian Spring,* a Piano Concerto, and varied works for solo instruments and piano

* Wrote two books, *The New Music,* and *Music and Imagination*

CHARLES IVES

* Born in U.S.A., 1874-1954

* Taught the fundamentals of music by his father

* Studied with Horatio Parker at Yale

* Made his living as an insurance agent

* Style was highly innovative, using bitonality, atonality, use of two different and clashing meters at once, quartertones

* Works include many songs, several of which use well known tunes or hymns arranged in 20th Century style; he also wrote piano sonatas, orchestral works, and chamber music

GEORGE GERSHWIN

* Born in U.S.A., 1898-1937

* Studied piano with Charles Hambitzer

* Studied composition with Henry Cowell and Joseph Schillinger

* Best known for combining "classical" forms with popular (especially jazz) style

* Famous works include *Rhapsody in Blue* for piano and orchestra, *An American in Paris* for orchestra, the opera *Porgy and Bess;* also wrote piano pieces and songs

Other 20th and 21st Century composers include:

Béla Bartók, born in Hungary, 1881-1945

Benjamin Britten, born in England, 1913-1976

Norman Dello-Joio, born in U.S.A., 1913-2008

Dmitri Kabalevsky, born in Russia, 1904-1987

Francis Poulenc, born in France, 1899-1963

Sergei Prokofiev, born in Russia, 1891-1953

Dmitri Shostakovich, born in Russia, 1906-1975

Igor Stravinsky, born in Russia, 1882-1971

1. List nine characterisitcs of music from the 20th and 21st Centuries and describe each.

a. _____

_____

b. _____

_____

c. _____

d. _____

e. _____

f. _____

g. _____

h. _____

i. _____

2. Complete the following information about each of these composers.

a. **Aaron Copland**

Dates of birth and death: _____

Historical Period: _____

Country of birth: _____

Education: _____

Positions held: _____

Style: _____

Compositions: _____

Books: _____

b. **Charles Ives**

Dates of birth and death: _____

Historical Period: _____

Country of birth: _____

Education: _____

Style of writing: _____

_____

Works: _____

_____

_____

c. **George Gershwin**

Dates of birth and death: _____

Historical Period: _____

Country of birth: _____

Education: _____

Style: _____

_____

Works: _____

_____

3. Name eight other 20th and 21st Century composers, their places of birth, and their dates of birth and death.

_____ _____ _____

_____ _____ _____

_____ _____ _____

_____ _____ _____

_____ _____ _____

_____ _____ _____

_____ _____ _____

_____ _____ _____

REVIEW
LESSONS 11-23

1. For each of the following phrases write the number of pulses in each measure, write counts between the treble clef and bass clef, and place accents on the strong beats.

   a. From *Invention No. 15* by J.S. Bach. _____ pulses per measure

   b. From *Sonata, Hob. XVI:40,* by Haydn. _____ pulses per measure

   c. From *Nocturne, Op. 55, No. 2,* by Chopin. _____ pulses per measure

2. Define each of the following terms.

a. atonality _____

b. exposition _____

c. fugue _____

d. enharmonic _____

e. parallel Major and minor _____

f. polytonality _____

g. suite _____

h. *ritenuto* _____

i. *scherzando* _____

j. syncopation _____

k. hemiola _____

l. *smorzando* _____

m. toccata _____

n. *sotto voce* _____

o. *rubato* _____

3. For each of the following examples, circle the compositional technique (repetition, imitation, sequence, canon, pedal point, augmentation, or diminution) and write the name of the technique on the line above the music.

a. From *Sonata, XVI:34*, by Haydn. _____

b. From *Sonata, XVI:34,* by Haydn. _____

c. From *Sonata, XVI:42,* by Haydn. _____

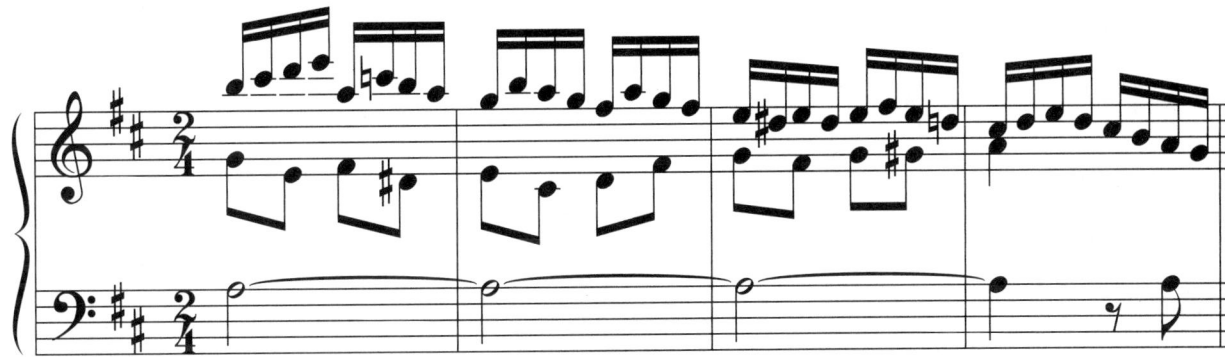

4. Name the texture used in each of the following examples.

a. From *Invention No. 15* by J.S. Bach. _____

b. From *Sonata, Hob. XVI:34,* by Haydn. _____

5. Name the three sections of Sonata form (Sonata Allegro form), and how the themes are used within each section.

_____   _____

_____   _____

_____   _____

6. Each of the following terms is associated with the Dance Suite or the Fugue. Match each term with the correct musical form.

a. Fugue   **b. Dance Suite**

_____ Subject   _____ Passapied   _____ Bouree

_____ Courante   _____ Loure   _____ Exposition

_____ Corrente   _____ Gavotte   _____ Minuet

_____ Polonaise   _____ Countersubject   _____ Gigue

_____ Sarabande   _____ Allemande   _____ Anglaise

_____ Air   _____ Episode

7. Match each of the following characteristics with the most appropriate historical period.

   a. Baroque   b. Classical   c. Romantic   d. Impressionsim   e. 20th & 21st Centuries

   _____ Sonata form developed

   _____ Use of ornamentation

   _____ Irregular and changing meters

   _____ Homophonic texture predominates

   _____ Lyric melodies

   _____ Programme music

   _____ Polyphonic texture in which harmonies are determined by the combinations of each individual line

   _____ Whole tone and pentatonic scales

   _____ Dance Suites

   _____ Serial music, Twelve Tone music

   _____ Harmonic structure and cadence points clearly defined

   _____ Atonality, Bitonality, and Polytonality

   _____ Colorful harmonies (within Major and minor tonalities)

   _____ Polyphonic texture (within Major and minor tonalities)

   _____ Alberti bass

8. For each of the following composers, name the historical period and the composer's dates, and write three important facts about the life of the composer.

Ludwig van Beethoven:

_____

_____

_____

Franz Liszt:

Claude Debussy:

Charles Ives:

Jean-Phillipe Rameau:

Arcangelo Corelli:

Wolfgang Amadeus Mozart:

Maurice Ravel:

Peter Ilyich Tchaikovsky:

Franz Josef Haydn:

Aaron Copland:

Henry Purcell:

_____
_____
_____

George Gershwin:

_____
_____
_____

Charles Griffes:

_____
_____
_____

Johannes Brahms:

_____
_____
_____

9. Transpose the following example to the key of f♯ minor.

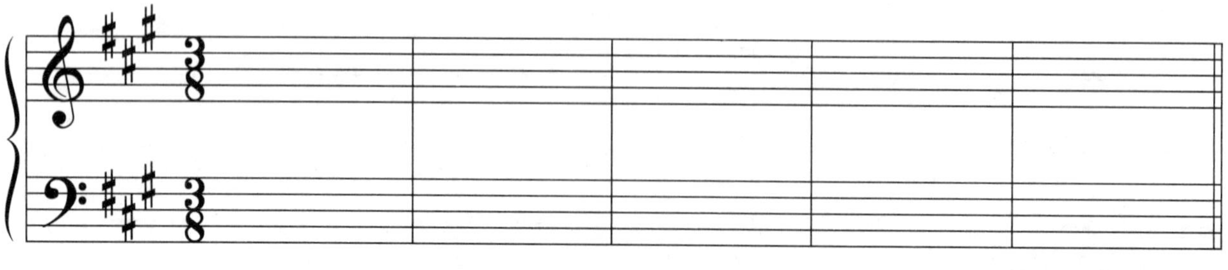

Burgmüller: *Ballade*

Score: _____ **REVIEW TEST** Perfect Score: 100
Passing Score: 70

1. Name each of the following intervals with its quality and number. (8 points)

   Melodic Intervals   Harmonic Intervals

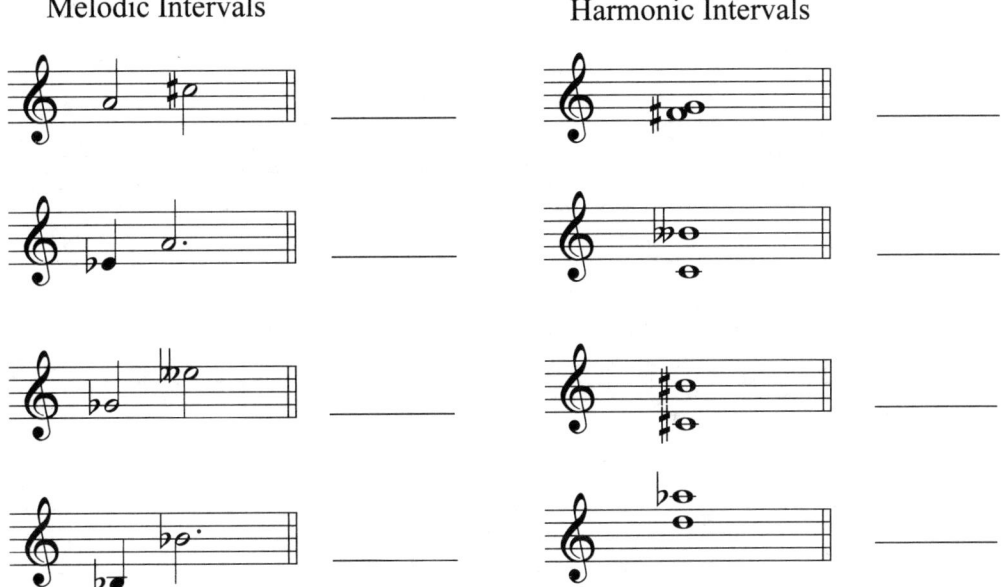

2. Write the name of the Major and minor key for each of the following key signatures. The first one is given. (8 points)

	Major Key	**Minor Key**
	F	d
	_____	_____
	_____	_____
	_____	_____
	_____	_____

3. Draw accidentals before the notes to complete each of the following melodies in the indicated keys. (5 points)

a. E Major

b. g melodic minor

c. f# natural minor

d. Whole Tone

e. b harmonic minor

4. Determine the time signature for each of the following rhythm patterns. (4 points)

a.

b.

c.

d.

5. Name the quality for each of the following seventh chords. Use the terms Dominant 7th, Major 7th, minor 7th, diminished 7th, and half diminished 7th. (6 points)

_____   _____   _____   _____   _____   _____

6. Write the name of the enharmonic equivalent for each of the following notes. (4 points)

E♭ _____   B _____   C♯ _____   F♭ _____

7. Match each of the following terms with its definition. (10 points)

_____ serial music

_____ modulation

_____ development

_____ fugue

_____ subject

_____ recapitulation

_____ atonality

_____ episode

_____ allemande

_____ parallel Major and minor

a. the main theme of a fugue

b. the third section of Sonata form

c. a style of writing in which several voices imitate each other

d. music in which a specific pattern, such as a twelve-tone row, rhythm, dynamics, or other musical element, is repeated throughout the composition

e. change of key

f. a section of a fugue in which the entire subject is not heard

g. a dance in moderate $\frac{4}{4}$ time with a short upbeat

h. Major and minor keys with the same letter name

i. the second section of Sonata form

j. no specific key or tonality

8. Match each of the following historical periods with the characteric with which it is associated. (5 points)

_____ Baroque   a. whole tone scales

_____ Classical   b. Sonata form

_____ Romantic   c. polytonality

_____ Impressionism   d. use of ornamentation

_____ 20th & 21st Centuries   e. lyric melodies

9. Answer the following questions about this musical example. (12 points)

1. Name the roots and qualities of the basic harmonies for measures 1-6.

Measure 1: _____   Measure 2: _____   Measure 3: _____

Measure 4: _____   Measure 5: _____   Measure 6: _____

2. What is the meaning of *piu lento*? _____

3. Is the key of this example well defined? _____

4. Give the Italian name and English meaning for the symbol *pp*. _____ _____

5. This example is from the same historical period as Bartók. Name two other composers from the same period. _____ _____

10. The following example is from *Sinfonia No. 7* by J.S. Bach. Answer the questions about the music. (12 points)

a. What is the key or tonality? _____ _____

b. How many main pulses are in each measure? _____

c. What is the texture? _____

d. Name each circled interval with its quality and number.

   1. _____ 2. _____ 3. _____ 4. _____

e. Name the root and quality of the chord on the second half of beat 2, measure 3.

   _____

f. Name the root and quality of the chord on beat 3 of measure 4. _____

g. Which historical period does J.S. Bach represent? _____

h. Name two other composers from this same period. _____ _____

11. The following example is from *Sonata, Hob. XVI:52* by Haydn. Answer the questions about the music. (14 points)

a. What is the key or tonality? _____ _____

b. What compositional technique is used in measures 2-3? _____

c. What compositional technique is used in measures 3-4? _____

d. How many main pulses are in each measure? _____

e. Name the three sections of Sonata form.

   _____   _____   _____

f. Name the root and quality of the seventh chord on beat 1 of measure 3. _____

g. Write the Roman Numerals and figured bass for measure 1, beats 2 and 3. _____ / _____   _____

   What is the name for this type of chord movement? _____ _____

h. Which historical period does Haydn represent? _____

i. Name two other composers from this same period. _____ _____

12. The following example is from *Intermezzo, Op. 118, No. 1,* by Brahms. Answer the questions about the music. (12 points)

a. What is the key or tonality? _____ _____

b. Name the root and quality of the seventh chord on beat 1 of measure 1. _____

c. Name the root and quality of the seventh chord on beat 1 of measure 6. _____

d. Name each circled interval with its quality and number.

   1. _____   2. _____   3. _____   4. _____

e. How many pulses are in each measure? _____

f. Which historical period does Brahms represent? _____

g. Name two other composers from this same period. _____ _____

REFERENCES

Apel, Willi. *Harvard Dictionary of Music, Second Edition.* Cambridge, Massachussetts: Belknap Press of Harvard University Press, 1972.

Arnold, Denis, ed. *The New Oxford Companion to Music, Volumes 1 and 2.* New York: Oxford University Press, 1983.

Music Teachers' Association of California. *Certificate of Merit Piano Syllabus.* San Francisco: Music Teachers' Association of California, 1992.

Music Teachers' Association of California. *Certificate of Merit Piano Syllabus.* Ontario, Canada: Frederick Harris Music Co., Limited, 1997.

Music Teachers' Association of California. *Certificate of Merit Piano Syllabus.* San Francisco: Music Teachers' Association of California, 2007.

Music Teachers' Association of California. *Certificate of Merit Piano Syllabus.* San Francisco: Music Teachers' Association of California, 2012.

Russell, John. *A History of Music for Young People.* Toronto, Canada: Clark, Irwin & Company Limited, 1965.

Sadie, Stanley, ed. *The New Grove Dictionary of Music and Musicians.* Washington, D.C.: Grove's Dictionaries of Music Inc., 1980.